FIGHTING YOUR BATTLES

JONATHAN EVANS

HARVEST HOUSE PUBLISHERS
EUGENE, OREGON

Scripture version credits appear at the back of the book

Cover design by Faceout Studio, Spencer Fuller

Cover photo © by subbery / Shutterstock

Interior design by Aesthetic Soup

For bulk, special sales, or ministry purchases, please call 1-800-547-8979.
Email: Customerservice@hhpbooks.com

This logo is a federally registered trademark of the Hawkins Children's LLC. Harvest House
Publishers, Inc., is the exclusive licensee of this trademark.

Fighting Your Battles
Copyright © 2022 by Jonathan Evans
Published by Harvest House Publishers
Eugene, Oregon 97408
www.harvesthousepublishers.com

ISBN 978-0-7369-8404-1 (pbk.)
ISBN 978-0-7369-8405-8 (eBook)

Library of Congress Control Number: 2022931567

Printed in the United States of America

22 23 24 25 26 27 28 29 30 / BP / 10 9 8 7 6 5 4 3 2 1

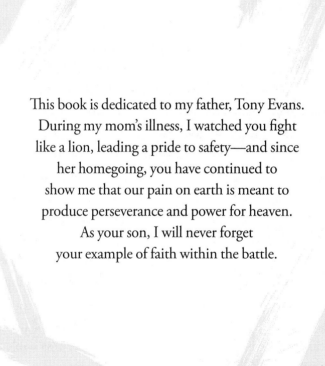

This book is dedicated to my father, Tony Evans.
During my mom's illness, I watched you fight
like a lion, leading a pride to safety—and since
her homegoing, you have continued to
show me that our pain on earth is meant to
produce perseverance and power for heaven.
As your son, I will never forget
your example of faith within the battle.

ACKNOWLEDGMENTS

Fighting Your Battles was a team effort from start to finish. I'd like to thank the following teammates who played key roles in helping me get this book across the goal line:

My wife, Kanika, who fights alongside me every day.

Our kids—Kelsey, Jonathan II, Kamden, Kylar, and Jade—who constantly remind me of God's love and purposes for me as one of His children.

The entire Evans family, including Dad and Mom, my sisters Chrystal and Priscilla, and my brother, Anthony. Even now, my inspiration comes from each of you. With your whole lives, you've taught me how to remain steadfast in every battle that God calls us to. Thank you for your commitment to Him and to me.

The entire Harvest House team, who are great partners and devoted co-laborers in God's kingdom. A special thanks to Bob Hawkins for his leadership, his friendship, and his belief in me as a preacher and author; Steve Miller, who had a real vision for this book and who, despite a very busy schedule of his own, was always available to offer wise editorial insight; and Kim Moore, who guided the manuscript through the design and production process.

Kris Bearss, who poured her heart and gifts into helping me develop and shape my spoken messages for a wider audience.

And last but definitely not least, my niece Kariss and her husband, Joshua Farris, for creating visual content for this book that will help inspire God's people to victory.

CONTENTS

EVERY CHRISTIAN'S PLAYBOOK FOR VICTORY

Everybody has some kind of battle. Everybody. My dad, pastor Tony Evans, has often told me, "You're either in a battle, on your way to a battle, or you just came out of one."

That's how life is. Trials and tribulations are headed your direction if they haven't shown up already. And like the mail you get in your box marked "Occupant," trouble doesn't care who lives where you live. But it has your address.

I've been going through some things recently for my own transformation. One of the hardest has been losing seven close family members to sudden death or long-term disease in less than two years, including my mom. I watched how bravely she fought cancer, how her faith sustained her and God strengthened her even as her body grew weaker. I've also seen what God has done to uphold me and my family in all of it.

Battles like these have really challenged me to think about what it means to fight God's way—relying on His power rather than my own. With this book, I want to process with you what I've been learning about the battles we all face. There are lessons that become clear only through trials and troubles. Those lessons gear us up to handle the hard times better, fight the good fight, and persevere toward the purpose God calls us to.

Already I can see that certain things are foundational.

Your victory starts with the battle. You might be saying, "I'm in this mess right now," but don't forget: the mess is the precursor to your miracle. Everybody who loves and serves God is going to go from test to testimony. That's the way of faith. First comes the battle, then the victory. The test strengthens your faith in Him; the victory solidifies your story with Him.

Battles are necessary in order to gain ground. In Bible times, tribes and nations often fought over acreage: they were either trying to add new land or defend their land from being taken away. We rarely go to war over physical property lines anymore, but spiritually we do. Emotionally we do. Relationally we do. In our lives and jobs and families and ministries, we are battling to protect and to progress what God has reserved for us.

God has new ground for you to gain, but it never comes easy. Battles must be fought. The land, the promises, and the experiences that are meant to be a part of your purpose only come as you stand and fight.

God is not wasteful. A common question in the heat of the struggle is why. *Why am I going through this?* Or *Why is this person I love having to go through this?*

"This" could be any hardship: illness, foreclosure, divorce, abuse, rejection, loneliness, depression, loss. God won't leave you empty, and He won't leave you behind. Those experiences are what He is using to build a future that will fulfill you and move His kingdom forward.

Knowing that He doesn't waste anything can help bring you through the valleys, as it's doing for me and my family.

God doesn't waste the things that overwhelm you.

He doesn't waste the things that beat you up.

He doesn't waste the trials that test you.

Is your pit extra deep right now? Has God allowed great misery to come to you? Then have hope: He intends great ministry *through* you. The depth of that hole often represents the height that God plans to take you.

We will get a deeper look at these truths and many others in this book. But every story I'll share here, and every Scripture we will study, has one main message: *Depend on God. All your battles belong to Him.* He says so in 2 Chronicles 20:15: "Do not fear or be dismayed because of this great multitude, for the battle is not yours but God's."

You and I are going to face enemies beyond what we can endure. Battles beyond what we can bear. Questions beyond what we can answer. All that opposition helps us recognize our need for the only One who can overcome on our behalf.

Whatever war you're in, brother…whatever struggle you're facing, sister…depend on God, who fights for you. He is able to do greater things in you and through you than you think are possible, because every battle of yours is actually His.

CHAPTER 1

FACING GIANTS

My wife, Kanika, and I put our son Jonathan II (we call him J2) in real football—tackle football—when he was eight. One reason I wanted to do that is because, at that age, the players are like cotton balls hitting each other, you know? I mean, eight-year-olds have on pads but they aren't tackling. They're basically hugging each other and trying to wrestle each other down. That's how they get used to the game.

I didn't want to wait until J2 was twelve to put him in real football because boys bring in a little more thunder then, and he probably would've walked away from the game. Still, even at eight years old, he was smart. He's a thinker. So when we got to the field where they were about to have their first game, J2 ran up there to check it all out. As soon as he got a look at the players on the other team, he said, "Dad, there are some big guys out here! They're bigger than me."

And the dad in me rose up. Anyone who knows me knows it wasn't "compassionate dad" eyeballing my son in that moment. It was "competitive dad," the one who played D1 and NFL football. "So what?" I said.

"No, Dad. Look…" J2 pointed to a couple of opposing players doing warm-ups. "Look how that kid catches the ball." Then his eyes bugged. "Look at how fast that other kid is!"

So, here was my son, standing on the sidelines analyzing his opponents before his very first game. I mean, he hadn't put his pads on, hadn't done any warmups, but already he was worried about the competition. The problem is, while he was busy analyzing his giants, he forgot himself. He forgot that he can catch anything thrown his way. That he's a natural athlete. That he is tall and rangy. And most of all, the dude has *wheels!*

I had to put *that* in front of his face—show him who he is—so *he* could remember and be ready for the game.

I'm using that analogy so you can think about your own life. When you're looking at a challenge in front of you, how do you see it? When life comes at you with some kind of giant, is your perspective based on your challenge or your calling? Do you perceive it as opposition or opportunity? Do you live your life based on the size of your problems or the size of your purpose?

Your calling is the full expression of the unique traits, gifts, and skills that God has embedded in you, including your passions and experiences. Every time you obediently bring all of who you are into the opportunities God gives you and the opposition the enemy throws at you, then you're operating in your calling. It's always for His glory and His game plan though, so that His kingdom keeps gaining ground. It's never simply for your advancement. Your advancement is just a secondary benefit of God's kingdom advancing.

Drafted!

In the Bible, I like David because he remembered who he was while facing all kinds of opponents. Everybody knows him as the underdog who took on an actual giant and won, but David could tell you a lot about overcoming family struggle too. He dealt with opposition at home, not just on the battlefield.

For starters, David was the youngest son in a big family. He was also the shortest dude among them—a "mini me" compared to his brothers. Between his youth and his size, nobody in his life took him seriously. Not even his own dad, Jesse. In fact, when the prophet Samuel showed up in Bethlehem to anoint the future king of Israel among Jesse's sons, the old man introduced Samuel to all his boys *except* David. They looked the part, tall and intimidating, just like Israel's current king, Saul. But we're told in 1 Samuel 16:14 that God's Spirit left Saul due to his disobedience. In other words, God had His eye out for different qualifications for Saul's successor.

The Lord wasn't thinking, *If My guy is at least 6'3", he'll be a real contender for the position.* No. God's focus was on traits like heart, humility, and faith. So once Samuel got to the end of the line and the Lord still hadn't said, "This is the one," the prophet asked, "Is there anybody else?"

What Jesse said was, "Well, yeah, I have one more son. My youngest. He's out in the pasture watching sheep…" However, I'm pretty sure David's dad was *wanting* to say, "But he's not your guy. He's only fifteen. He's no taller than a fence post. And he writes poems and music out there under the stars. Not what I'd consider a good prospect for king."

If David's own father disqualified him, why wouldn't everybody disqualify him? If David's own father didn't think his youngest son had a chance of being picked to replace King Saul, who would? Yet the Lord told Samuel, "Arise, anoint him; for this is he" (16:12).

With your choosing comes your calling. The God who chose David for His team is the God who chooses you. The difference is, once you're on the Lord's team, you don't just remain a player in His eyes. You become family. To paraphrase Ephesians 1, "You're chosen. You're blessed. You're adopted. You're redeemed" (verses 3-7).

With your choosing will also come your challenges, and those challenges are the stage on which to display what you've been chosen to do—win! You are called to overcome anything and anyone who stands against you. Your last name becomes Victory, not Victim.

In order for you to remember and be ready for *your* battles, God puts verses like these in front of you—to show you who you are:

- 1 John 5:4, "For whoever has been born of God overcomes the world."

- John 16:33, [Jesus said,] "In the world you have tribulation, but take courage; I have overcome the world."

- Romans 8:37, "We overwhelmingly conquer through Him who loved us."

- Romans 8:30, "These whom [God] predestined, He also called; and these whom He called, He also justified; and these whom He justified, He also glorified."

What we see in David here in 1 Samuel 16, just after he's been called, can also be seen throughout his life if you read his entire story: *from our calling comes our confidence.* The calling is key because who you are overrides whoever you're up against. You might be up against someone who claimed to be your friend but isn't acting like it. You might be up against a hostile boss, a hater on social media, an unethical business competitor, or even your own family. Whoever is standing against you, God is backing you. He has picked you. And now, as one of His chosen ones, you have access to all the team's resources: the coaching, the support, the camaraderie—and the winningest Playbook in the universe, the Word of God. Even more so, you have inherited every bit of power and authority that comes with the family name. But it also means you're expected to live like it.

That's a lot of pressure if you're trying to do it on your own.

Thankfully, we don't have to go it alone. The ones He calls are the ones He equips. The ones He calls are the ones He readies: "Then Samuel took the horn of oil and anointed him in the midst of [David's] brothers. And the Spirit of the LORD rushed upon David from that day forward" (1 Samuel 16:13 ESV).

The Spirit of the Lord was on him. From that day forward. That's the difference in any Christian's life.

Nobody took David seriously except for God. But right there was David's advantage. He may have been short on inches, but David's faith towered above everybody else's because *the Spirit of the Lord was on him.* He was sure of the Source of his strength. He knew the Spirit's supply would never fail. All of this gave him a courage like no one else. "From where does my help come?" he would write later. "My help comes from the LORD" (Psalm 121:1-2).

His Power, His Presence

Fast forward a few years. David has been splitting his time between tending his father's flocks and serving in Saul's court as his lead musician. One day, Jesse asks David to take food supplies to his three oldest brothers, who were all serving in Saul's army against the Philistines. David reaches the Israelite camp just as the two armies are drawing up for another day of battle on opposite sides of the Valley of Elah. That's when the show starts.

The Philistines' nine-foot killing machine, Goliath, comes out of his tent and shouts across the valley, daring anyone from Israel to fight him. He's been doing this for forty days straight, his deep voice echoing off those hills. He doesn't just strut around either. He's all armored up in bronze for a little extra intimidation factor, with an armor bearer by his side carrying Goliath's massive spear.

I had never really thought this through before, but that armor bearer held Goliath's spear until he needed it. That told me, not only is this problem big, but this problem likes to show off. The giant was showing off. And the guys on the frontlines believed the act. They turned and ran for cover, every single time. *Game over before it's begun.*

Of course this made Goliath even cockier. Like any bully, he kept amping things up, cursing God and mocking the army of God's people…on and on and on.

It wasn't just Saul's men, though. Not even Saul himself was willing to take on the Philistine champion of war. You know what the ruler of Israel said? The same thing my son said when he got a look at some of the other team's players: "Whoa! Do you see that guy? See how big he is? He can't lose!"

Every time we as God's people back down, the giant grows bigger in our eyes. And as our problem grows bigger, the God we serve seems smaller and smaller.

That's why courage needs a calling, so that we don't forget. So that we stop ourselves and say, "Hey, wait a minute! I'm a warrior in the army of the living God—and a member of the ruling family!" God's calling on us means His power is in us anytime we face a giant. God's calling on us means His power goes with us into every battle. And where His power is, His presence is.

But we have to remember. David remembered. As soon as he heard Goliath's words, he was mad. Fighting mad. "Let me at him!"

His brothers rolled their eyes. *Little bro, tryin' to be a big man and prove himself.* What those boys didn't understand is that David wasn't out to prove what he could do. He was out to prove what God could do.

The monstrous call that God has placed *on you* means that God has giants to defeat *through you*. So when you break huddle and head into the game, you'd better break huddle concerned about the call way more than the problem, understanding that the reason you have a problem—the reason you're facing a giant—is because you have a call.

The bigger your problem, the bigger your call.

I remember the first time my siblings and I heard about my mom's diagnosis. The doctors knew there was nothing else they could do to save her life; they just didn't know how long she would live. It could be three months to six months. It could be a year to a year and a half. But it wouldn't be long. Looking at the test results, their timelines differed, but they all agreed, "You're going to lose, Mrs. Evans."

When Mom saw our reactions, she went straight to "Whoa, this is spiritual warfare. We've got to remember what we're up against." She was fully aware that the real battle wasn't going to be the physical one. Tough as that might be, she was being called to a fight of faith, and she reminded my dad and each of us kids of this.

That's the kind of people we need to be around—people with hearts that listen to God instead of what the doctors say or what our enemy looks like. We can't let the giant's shouts or threats make us run from our calling. That was my mom's charge to us as a family: Don't stare at the giant so much that you tuck tail and run from what God has called you to. Champions hold their ground and fight.

Let me ask you again: As you're surveying the field of your life, what's your perspective from where you're standing? Is your perspective based on your problem or your calling? On your struggle or your supply? Are you seeing the size of your opponent, or the size of your opportunity with God's Spirit in you?

A Position Change

In a good way, David's perspective throughout his life was just crazy. His attitude was, "I see what you're seeing, but I don't see it like you see it!" His dad and his brothers doubted him, Saul would doubt him, and Goliath would doubt him. It didn't matter. David's faith was in God. He was counting on the One who called him.

If you see only the obstacle in front of you, you'll let the obstacle overtake you. You'll be a complainer, not a victor. A doubter, not a warrior. David remembered both his calling and his covering. His story is about a change in position as well as perspective.

With every giant, our approach changes as our position changes. As we become more sure of who we are in Christ, we see more and more who our giant isn't. This is what caused David to say, "Who is this uncircumcised Philistine, that he has dared to defy the armies of the living God?" (1 Samuel 17:26). David was covered under God's covenant with Israel.

As a baby, my youngest niece, Kariss, was scared of the family dog, Solomon. To her the dog was a beast, you know? Never mind that Solomon was a poodle.

Solomon was a poodle in every way—nothing ferocious about him. But because Kariss was little, she'd go wild and scream, "Poppy! Poppy! Pick me up!" as soon as the dog came her way.

One day, my dad picked her up with Solomon still barking. My niece looked at the dog…and looked back at Poppy. She looked at the dog…looked at Poppy…looked at the dog, and all of a sudden you could see the light go on. She busted out giggling, "Na nah, na nah, na nah!" at Solomon.

Her whole approach changed. You know why? Because her position changed. She realized the significance of her grandfather's arms. Being in the arms of her Poppy changed how she looked at her problem.

The problem was still there—the dog didn't stop barking, and Goliath didn't stop taunting either. But Kariss and David were covered. They were safe.

The problem isn't the problem. But in order to not be controlled by your problem, you have to have a perspective that comes from a certain position. David had this confidence: *I'm a child of God. My head has been anointed with oil. His Spirit is on me. I have a covenant with God, and my people have a covenant with God.*

At the same time, he was seeing that the armor, the armor bearer, the big weapons—none of that stuff could protect Goliath. To David, the fact that his challenger was not circumcised meant a whole lot more than everything else people were looking at. *He's not under the covenant.*

That's what circumcision represented to the people of Israel: being in covenant with God. That's where all those New Testament Scriptures of being an overcomer—a justified, glorified, chosen, and redeemed child of God—come in. It all has to do with your covenant with God and His covenant with you. Once you've dedicated yourself to the Lord, you are covered by His dedication to you.

Goliath was not in covenant with God. Neither were his people. They did not have the promises of the Lord. So Goliath was vulnerable in ways he didn't realize. David's covering, on the other hand, was impenetrable. He was completely safe.

So are you, child of God. Your problem is hovering over you. It's a big storm cloud. The lightning is striking, the thunder is rolling, and you're in a downpour. What's your approach, your response? Are you thinking about the problem or your position? If you're busy thinking about the storm and what it's whipping at you, then the problem is controlling your entire approach. You'll be drowning in the problem.

My family and I could have drowned as Mom got sicker. The

rain came hard and fast. Yet God lets every one of His sons and daughters know that, based on Jesus' work and God's anointing in your life, you are in position to come through any storm and over-power any giant. It may be raining, but pop open the umbrella of God's covenant and understand that, even though there's a storm, you're covered.

Go with God

Contrast David's approach with Saul's. Saul was the king of God's covenant people, and he knew the Philistines were uncir-cumcised. Still, Saul was worried. Not only was David small for his age, but he was too young for battle. (In ancient Israel, you had to be twenty to enlist.) The king actually told David, "You are not able to go against this Philistine to fight with him; for you are but a youth, and he has been a man of war from his youth" (17:33 ESV).

Goliath was ranked number one in the world. He'd been fighting wars since before David was born. So Saul was right, *David* couldn't win. But the kid knew how to get the win: "The LORD...will deliver me from the hand of this Philistine," he told Saul (verse 37 ESV).

In other words, *God is able.* We are not.

David had gotten the memo.

Next, Saul offered David his own armor. Basically, he tried to make *David* bigger. Isn't that our go-to as we size up the giants from the sidelines? Isn't that how we prepare for battle in our own strength? We try to make ourselves (or our guy) seem bigger. We think, *If I just had more money, more influence, more followers and views and members, more, more, more, maybe then I'll have a better chance of victory.* Saul obviously thought the same way we do.

Saul loaded David up, even handing over his brass helmet and his sword. The shepherd-singer must have looked like a three-year-old trying to put on an NFL uniform. No way could he fight in that!

Instead, David opted to go to battle in the greatness of the One who called him. He decided he would rely on that to defeat Goliath.

Grabbing his slingshot, David picked up a few small stones and headed toward the Philistine camp. The kid who couldn't carry a warrior's weights—he would be the one to face the giant. The rookie with faith like a rock—he would take the field with the confidence of Super Bowl champion Tom Brady.

How could he? He remembered his calling. *I'm more than a conqueror.* He remembered his covering. I can imagine David telling himself, "If God says this is who I am, and He's got my back, then how can I not take on this giant He has called me to fight?"

It didn't matter who or what he was up against. David was set. He would go with God, and God would go with him.

Remember Your Testimony

Not only do we need to keep our call in front of us and our covering over us, but we can't forget our testimony. Our testimony is what God did for us and through us in the past. What we saw God do yesterday produces boldness for today.

David was full of confidence for this exact reason: He'd seen the Lord's track record throughout his life.

What was David's job before he became Israel's king? Tending sheep. What's the job of a shepherd? He has to lead the sheep. Protect them. Provide for them. And yes, clean up their messes. So when Saul told him, "You can't fight Goliath; you're just a kid," David referred to his past job as a keeper of his father's sheep: "The LORD who delivered me from the paw of the lion and from the paw of the bear will deliver me from the hand of this Philistine" (verse 37 ESV).

David had no doubt that the One who had called him to the battle would fight for him in the midst of it. David had no doubt that the One who had shown up for him every time in the past was going to be in the battle with him now.

In *your* battle today, you can't forget what God has already brought you through.

When it was time for David to go up against Goliath, 1 Samuel 17:48 says, "David ran quickly toward the battle line to meet the Philistine." He ran toward the battle because, even though this challenger was bigger than the lion and the bear, David's God was the Almighty, the Lord of heaven and earth, the faithful Deliverer who never fails. The Lord would do again what the Lord has always done.

Listen, the challenge in front of you is the stairway to your promotion. Don't let whatever is standing in your way force you to miss the next level.

God often likes to promote us in the challenge before He promotes us in the calling. In other words, there's a job interview before you get the job. It's as if He's saying, "I have to know if you're going to remain faithful. If you're going to continue to trust Me by faith, not by sight, with the beast that is staring you down right now."

At the beginning of J2's football season the following year, his team was going up against the same opponent. So I showed him his game from the previous year to help him remember, *You're being promoted today.* My point was: The reason you see a bigger challenge, son? The reason the opponent looks bigger now than before? It's because you have a bigger call.

If you think about that in your own life—if you think about who God says you are and the things you've already been able to accomplish because of His work through you—then you realize, *Okay! Let me pass this test so I can reach the next level that God is calling me to.*

At the Frontlines

Just because you recognize your calling doesn't mean the giant goes away. It just means that you recognize, *My calling is bigger than my giant.*

When David showed up at the valley carrying only a slingshot, Goliath took one look and laughed. That's what the old pros do. First Samuel 17:42 (NIV) says the veteran of war felt disdain, for David was "little more than a boy." A boy with no spear, no armor, nothing. *Obviously a rookie.*

What happens to rookies? They get put in their place. They get initiated. So Goliath starts talking trash and throwing shade at David and everyone he represents.

David didn't blink. He knew whose jersey he was wearing. "You come to me with a sword and with a spear and with a javelin," he said, "but I come to you in the name of the LORD of hosts, the God of the armies of Israel, whom you have defied. This day the LORD will deliver you into my hand, and I will strike you down and cut off your head."

God's warrior wasn't done. "I will give the dead bodies of the host of the Philistines this day to the birds of the air and to the wild beasts of the earth, that all the earth may know that there is a God in Israel, and that all this assembly may know that the LORD saves not with sword and spear. For the battle is the LORD's, and he will give you into our hand" (verses 45-47 ESV).

Again and again right here he says, "The Lord will do it. The Lord. The Lord. It's not up to me." Anytime you see something repeated in a Scripture passage, pay attention. It's important. It means, *This is for real! Something big is happening.*

We all know what happens next. Goliath steps toward David, David runs at Goliath, slings one stone—and down the giant goes. Verse 49 says, "The stone sank into his forehead, and he fell on his face to the ground."

You see that? Goliath fell on his face.

To the ground.

Dead.

In verse 50, we're reminded, "David prevailed over the Philistine with a sling and with a stone…There was no sword in the hand of David." God's power, not manpower.

What David saw as he analyzed his opponent is what we have to see: the size of our giant doesn't compare to the size of our God. That's the game-changer. If the Spirit of the Lord is with us, then He is on us, in us, over us, behind us, and before us. That means we take God's power and presence onto the field as we fight.

Think about your own life and the giant you're up against. How are you seeing it?

Whichever giant you're staring at right now, you're going to find the courage to face it in remembering. In remembering your calling, your covering, and your testimony. As I've said, remembering God doesn't remove the giant. It just means you recognize that the God who goes with you is bigger than the giant who opposes you.

His Battle

"The battle is the LORD's." Those were David's words (verse 47), but they have to be our battle cry too. Every battle we will ever face belongs to God.

In those times when the battle really beats you up and you get overwhelmed, it's usually for one of two reasons: Either you're running into the fight on your own power or you've tried to own what isn't yours.

Running toward the giant without God's power is going to get you crushed. By yourself, you simply don't possess what's necessary in order to overcome. I don't; David didn't; my family didn't. With God, however, every one of us possesses what's necessary. We must enter the battle in His power.

The second reason we can end up overwhelmed is because we've taken the ownership role instead of the stewardship role. You and I are supposed to be stewards of the battle, not owners of the battle. So recognize who really owns it. This is one of those statements that takes the monkey off people's backs. The One who owns it is Lord over it. The Owner has the power. He can defeat anyone or anything that comes against Him or His people.

No matter what others think, the battle is the Lord's. No matter what the giant says about you, no matter how your family or your boss might doubt you, you cannot lose if the fight is His. You might look like a flea compared to the giant you're up against, but looks don't win.

The God of heaven and earth is with you. The Warrior of all the ages fights for you. The battle is the Lord's.

Your victory is sure.

CHAPTER 2

THIRSTY

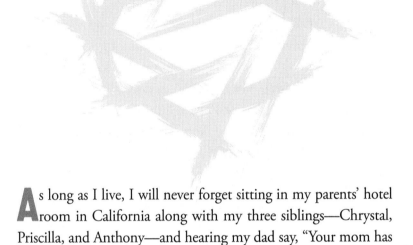

As long as I live, I will never forget sitting in my parents' hotel room in California along with my three siblings—Chrystal, Priscilla, and Anthony—and hearing my dad say, "Your mom has cancer."

Many of you know how that feels. Everything changes when you get that kind of news. To me it felt like somebody had just rubbed Icy Hot all over me. I was hot, cold, sweating, and shivering, all at the same time.

Things change further when your dad—the man who has always found a way to figure things out—takes off to the far end of the room in tears because there is nothing his hands can do about the situation.

Tony Evans likes to fix things. He likes to be able to make things happen. But in this situation, there wasn't much he could do other than go to God.

Priscilla and Anthony ran over to console my dad, and they all cried together. Mom was sitting there looking at Dad, then us, concerned about how we would absorb this hit alongside the deaths and illnesses of other family members.

"I understand that you're sad about this news," she said. "I understand that we're going through a lot as a family. Right now, we're in this season of over and over and over…"

That's what she called it: a season of "over and over and over."

I looked at Exodus 17 during that time, and I tell you, I could sympathize with the people of Israel. Because after a while, after enough things happen "over and over and over," you really start wondering whether or not the Lord is with you.

In Exodus 17, the people of Israel were asking that exact question: "Is the Lord with us or not?"

No Water

You know why they asked? Because the Lord had told them to leave Egypt. It was the Lord who had made big promises about a promised land. Who had raised up this big-time leader named Moses. Who had produced these big-time plagues in order to free His people from the Egyptians. All for what?

To bring them to the middle of a *desert*?

Verses 1-3 say that it was also the Lord who commanded the Israelites to camp at a place named Rephidim. "Camp" means that you want to be revitalized. You want to sit down and restore your mojo because you've got a long road ahead. The people had their Vitamixes out, hoping to get some juice for the journey. The problem is, God told them to camp where there was no water.

Can you imagine walking from Africa through the Middle East without water? They were in the wilderness, experiencing that dry mouth you get when you eat that honeybun on a July afternoon in Texas but can't find anything to wash it down with—only this was worse. It wasn't some pattycake issue. For them, this was life or death. They had to be thinking, *What? But we're just doing what You said, Lord!*

They were being triple obedient:

- Going in the direction God had called them.
- Following Moses, God's choice to lead them.
- Camping where they were told to camp.

And yet here they were, about to die of thirst.

Many of you have had that disappointment. You thought that if you just slowed down and focused on your marriage, the two of you would get your mojo back. Instead, your relationship is worse. You thought that if you tried that new thing in your business or ministry (the thing you were sure God had green-lighted), the risk would be worth it. But somehow the outlook is still gloomy and gray.

The expectation is what messes you up. The expectation is that if you're camping, *Alright! I'm getting ready for the next phase.* You feel hope for right now and hope for what's ahead. But then you come to the campsite, and you find yourself in a place with no water, about to die of thirst.

After hearing the news about my mom, I remember having that doubt inside: *We were going in the direction You called us to, God. But Uncle Bo passed away. Aunt Bev passed away. Wynter passed away. Two-Daddy [my dad's dad] is struggling to eat. We've got a diagnosis on my mom...C'mon now, Jesus—can You give us a break? You are the one who told us to camp. We're only doing what You asked us to do.*

Bad things don't happen just when you're outside the Lord's will, doing the opposite of what He says. Sometimes bad things happen *when* you're following Him!

I'm sure Moses wished he could tell the people, "Just follow God to the Promised Land and everything will be fine." I wish *I* could tell you that if you hang out with Jesus, your life will be all good. But sometimes, it's not until you're going in the direction God has called you that suffering comes your way.

Looking at both the Old and New Testaments, you find a lot of suffering. Really, that's the Bible's theme. It's a book of suffering… Job. Abraham and his long journey to an unknown land. Women like Sarah, Rebekah, Rachel, Hannah, and Elizabeth and their years of barrenness. The future king David having to escape Saul's efforts to kill him. Jesus' disciples enduring beatings and prison for sharing the gospel. And Jesus Himself, the one who was without sin, hanging on a cross. All those people suffered while following God. All those people suffered while trying to do what God called them to do.

That's what we find in Exodus 17 too.

So I want to start off making sure we understand that following Jesus often means you *will* suffer. It means being put in a position where you're going to have to trust Him.

That's where my wife and I were awhile back. We were on our knees, needing more faith, after two miscarriages. We were so excited to have kids. We love kids, we wanted kids, and we knew that God loves kids. But in the process of trying to have kids, Kanika and I had two miscarriages, and then another two.

To not really know if we could have children—to not really know if being parents was something God meant for us—was devastating. We weren't so sure that we could trust God through it. After a while, we both started wondering, *Hey God, we're following You. We're doing what You've asked. Are You with us or not?*

Complaints from Camp

Once the people of Israel saw they had no water, they began to grumble and complain. I used to read about them and judge, "Y'all! Don't you see what God did for you yesterday? You don't remember?

It was like a chapter ago, you know? Remember the escape from Egypt? The Red Sea? The manna? Not a big time lapse! So why y'all complaining?" But then when you go through it yourself, you're like, "Oh! Now I understand."

I mean, this was a place where they expected to be revitalized, right? *God brought us here, to this exact location!* Yet they were staring at nothing but sand. Then there was the escape from Egypt. *Pretty frightening.* And the Red Sea? *That was a close call. We could've died if Pharaoh's army had caught up to us!* And the manna and quail— *Well, yeah, but the Lord waited until we were nearly starving before He even sent those.*

I don't condone complaining at all, but at least they were complaining about big stuff. We mostly complain about small stuff.

By the time they camped at Rephidim and saw no water anywhere, that was it. They'd had it. "Why is it that you have brought us up from Egypt?" they grumbled to Moses. "To kill us and our children and our livestock with thirst?" (see Exodus 17:3).

All I can say is, *you* try being in their position. *You* try walking through a desert carting everything you own and ending up at camp with not a drop of refreshment in sight. It seems like complaining is something any of us would do.

Of course the people turned to Moses for help: "Can you give us something to drink? After all this walking, how about some water?"—to which he replied, "I'm looking around, guys, but we don't have any water."

Right then, things went downhill fast. They got so angry, they picked up rocks to stone their leader. I mean, it was bad. Because when you feel like things are tanking, you try to figure out whose fault it is. And the first place you look is to the top, the guy in charge.

"Hey, Mo, if you aren't going to do something about this, we'll have to!"

Verse 3 says they were grumbling at Moses, but really, they were questioning God: "Are You with us? You say we're headed to our destiny, Lord. So how is it that we're dehydrated? If we're on our way to a promise, then how is it that we don't have a provision? Why would You bring us to this absolute nowhere?"

It's just like us to do that, to complain and lash out when God apparently isn't providing. But do you know what complaints really are? They're concerns that God is not present with us. They're our way of saying, "I thought God knows what He's doing, but He obviously doesn't. Maybe His way and His plan aren't worth trusting after all."

But God had His chosen people there, in that place, for a reason. He was trying to show them how to trust Him in season and out of season.

C'mon, Jesus!

If you and I can just be real with each other, we've asked the same things as the Israelites were. *How can I be following the One who is the Living Water and still be thirsty? How am I sitting here in desolation as I'm following the Lord to my so-called destiny? C'mon Jesus!*

Maybe right now is one of those times in your life. You're camped in the desert, and you're thirsty for God to come through in your marriage, your finances, in some big career decision. You're following God, but thirsty. You're in the middle of nowhere, and thirsty.

You're so desperate for Him to break through, but He doesn't seem to be who He says He is. *God, are You able?*

You need a break from this season of "over and over and over," but nothing is turning out how you expected. You're worn out, you're dehydrated…and it's been a long journey already. *God? You there?*

For some of us, if we're honest, there's even more to it than that.

Things are bad enough that you're doubting whether God is real. Or whether He's good.

If you're experiencing any of these scenarios, open up your Bible and read through the entire chapter of Exodus 17. If you have time, go back even further and read chapters 14 through 17.

In Exodus 14, God's people were caught between a rock and a hard place, with the Red Sea in front of them and Pharaoh behind them. Chapter 15 was the first time they didn't have water. In chapter 16, they needed some manna. Chapter 17, they don't have water again.

It's one thing after another. Over and over and over.

Sit in that as you read. Again, I don't condone complaining, but I do understand. I see their situation and say, "Man, can you believe they're following God, and they don't know whether they're going to live or die?"

The reason I went to this passage during my own dry season is because I was thinking, *Jesus, c'mon! My family and I are just doing what You asked us to do. Why can't we get a break? Where's the water in our camp?* So I'm feeling them, the people of Israel. Aren't you? I'm like, "Yeah, I'm with you, because God told you to go there, and Jesus is the Living Water...so He says in John 4. So what's with all this thirst?"

It can get confusing sometimes. But I had to caution myself, because that "C'mon, Jesus" can soon become a demand, like He owes me something. I start talking like I'm entitled, while God is saying, "This isn't a business transaction. I'm trying to take you somewhere."

Once Moses saw the people tossing the rocks, he said, "C'mon, Jesus!" I just know he did! He said, "God, we're not trying to die today. Can You do something about this? The people are thirsty. You told us to camp here. Don't make me look bad. We're on our way to the Promised Land. But everyone is at their breaking point."

Right on Time

God came through at their breaking point. Just in the nick of time. You'll find that in Exodus 17, in verses 5 through 7. He told Moses, "Go to Mount Horeb and strike that rock with My staff, and water will come through."

At the breaking point, when the people were ready to give up on God...

when the people were about to turn their backs on God...

when they were about to lose faith because they couldn't take any more suffering and their essential needs weren't being met...right then and there, Moses got a word from the Lord: "Now mosey on up to Mount Horeb. You go up there and make sure you take the staff of God with you."

Moses did as God commanded, and the water just flowed. It was enough water for the whole nation of Israel, including their livestock!

Do you know what that scene represents? We'll talk more about it in a coming chapter, but going to the rock with the staff of God represents relying on the spiritual realm within our earthly experiences. Moses drew down the power of heaven into the camp at Rephidim. When you go up and strike that rock in obedience to God's command, taking Him at His word, you will no longer thirst. God may not give you water exactly when you want it or when you think you need it, but He gives it right on time.

Have you ever experienced God breaking through in the nick of time? He likes doing that, doesn't He? (Though I like for Him to show up a little before that!) But I think He waits sometimes because He wants His people knowing that right when we're about to give up on Him, He hasn't given up on us. He is readying you for where He is taking you, just like He is readying me for where He is taking me.

Without faith it's impossible to please the Lord (see Hebrews

11:6). He breaks out the water at your wit's end, not just so you can continue the journey but so you can learn to trust Him as your journey continues.

Some of you are in that phase where it's just "I'm thirsty," and nothing else. Zero provision anywhere you look. But God says, "Those who wait for the Lord will gain new strength" (Isaiah 40:31), not those who don't.

You have to wait.

There will be times when you say to yourself, "C'mon, Jesus. I'm doing what You told me to do. You brought me here." Some of you are reading this and thinking, *Man, I might be better just going back to my old life. It might be better for me to go back to my old way of operating because there's nothing for me here.* But don't forget:

In chapter 14 you were between a rock and a hard place, yet the sea opened.

In chapter 15 you needed water. It was provided.

In chapter 16 you were hungry, and manna fell from heaven. (A little bit too much quail maybe, but at least the manna was in the right portion!)

So in this chapter, what are you complaining about?

See, the enemy is happy to let us focus so hard on our current problem that we don't remember how great God has been in our past. We're quick to forget. But the water came down once Moses struck the rock.

Right when the people were about to give up, Moses reached up, and there was water. They received God Water. That's way better than the water we have. The water that came from that rock—it had to be the best stuff ever. It was from *the* Source, not the city water department.

I remember being at a breaking point financially at Christmastime one year and having to figure this waiting stuff out.

I sometimes dabble in real estate, and one day I decided, *You know what? I'm going to try flipping some houses.* So I got out there and worked it the wrong way. Soon I was out of money, with two houses for sale and the holidays getting close.

My kids were little at that time, and they were bringing their Christmas lists to me, but the houses weren't selling because it wasn't the right time of year. My wife was looking at me, silently asking, "What are you going to do?" I had literally no idea how else to make those sales happen for my family. I just kept thinking, *I don't know if you're getting anything for Christmas, kids, because Daddy was watching too much HGTV and got in a little over his head.*

I was so stressed trying to pay two water bills, two electric bills, two of everything. I hired different realtors, trying to get these deals done, but the reality is, I was extremely dehydrated in this situation and there was no water to be found. But I did pray. I was totally dependent, asking God to come through.

I had to depend on God because I couldn't handle my situation by myself. But I also wasn't sure if God would come through. I started complaining and wondering whether the Lord was really with me, because being a father and not being able to provide gifts for my kids was just about as bad as I could imagine.

December 1 comes, and I'm really nervous.

December 15, and those houses are still for sale.

Here comes December 20, and I am sweating.

Lo and behold, just as I was about to give up and tell my kids, "Hey, we can't do any gifts this Christmas," an investor comes to me and says, "I see the two houses you have on the market. I want to buy them both—cash. I can close in three days."

We close on December 23. I get all my money back from those deals and then some.

December 24, my wife and I go to the store and shop for presents.

And on December 25, our children have no idea what happened because all their gifts are sitting under the tree.

God has a way of coming through at a breaking point to let you know that He is your Source. The One who provides. You may have to wait for the water though, longer than you might like. It's as if He's waiting until you're at your wit's end before He heals your situation and reminds you: I am still God.

Living in the Know

Where in your life are you feeling dehydrated? Where are you saying, "God, I'm being obedient, but are You with me or not?"

Let me encourage you to continue to trust God through it, because there is a promised land ahead. There is a destiny. A goal. He is taking you somewhere that maybe only He sees in this moment. It may be nowhere on your radar. But it's on His.

My kids are always extremely disappointed when they ask for something and I say no, or when they go a long time without something they really want. They haven't learned to live in "the know" of their father because they can't see what I can see. They only know what they want in the moment.

Understand, though, that God sees. He sees where He is taking you. He sees the finish line over in Canaan. He sees your destiny and your purpose, and He is bringing all of it together.

For you men out there who feel like you're in a stoning situation—you're trying to lead your family in righteousness so that the promises of God can be on your household, but rocks are being thrown because circumstances aren't measuring up to expectations—I encourage you to have faith and keep believing. Keep being the man God has biblically called you to be and doing what He has biblically called you to do.

And for you women who are having to be the leader because

either no man is there or because the man that *is* there isn't leading, I encourage you to continue to be a 1 Peter 3 woman—respectful and pure in conduct, leading by example despite the trial. God is taking you somewhere, and at every step, He will remain your Source.

Stay true, you hear? Be steadfast in your deserts and continue to abound in the work of the Lord, because I'm telling you: He will come through. Don't give up on Him. He will never give up on you.

CHAPTER 3

FIGHTING GOD'S WAY

One thing we can be certain of in the Christian life is that everyone who follows God will face battles. Just thinking about that can be discouraging. So let me share another defining moment from Exodus 17 that has encouraged me in my battles. I want you to have the same kind of encouragement in your battles.

The passage begins, "Then Amalek came and fought against Israel at Rephidim" (verse 8). *Then* is a common transition word in Scripture, along with *therefore*. When you see a *therefore*, don't just keep reading; you need to back up and see what the *therefore* is there for. In the same way, *then* is signaling us: "Don't start here; go back and look at what happened *before* then, because this is all connected."

So what happened just before verse 8? In verses 1-7, we saw God's people set up camp in the desert at Rephidim. Although that's where He told them to camp, it was a place with no water. The people complained and nearly rioted against Moses, fearing they would die of thirst, but just in time, God delivered water from a rock. At Israel's breaking point, when the people were really questioning, "Is God with us or not?"—God answered.

I can see them now, can't you? They went to the Desert Walmart and got the party cups. You know those red ones? It was party time! Men, women, and children dipped their cups in that God Water, and suddenly they felt revitalized. Their thirst was quenched. They had proof—right there in their hands—that God was with them after all.

That's when verse 8 happens: "Then Amalek came and fought against Israel at Rephidim."

You know those times? They make you do a double take: *Wait a minute now. I just got something to drink, God! I just got a break. How is it that, when You show up and I'm feeling like I've gotten my faith back, I look over my shoulder and here's somebody wanting to fight? Man, if it's not this, it's that. If it's not her, it's him. How am I supposed to get a jump on my future with one problem after another in my present?*

I felt some of that not too long ago. I'd made some extra money from a speaking engagement—the organization had given me an honorarium of five hundred dollars for my time. So I went to Discount Tire to get my "free" tire rotation, and right away they're telling me, "Your tires are bald. You need four new ones."

"How much is that?" I asked.

"Five hundred dollars."

As soon as I came up, having a little extra money to spare, I went right back down. You know how that feels. It seems like the minute you get blessed, something shows up to take you right back to where you started.

Same Old, Same Old

Not only did Amalek break up the party, but he came *to Rephidim*. Don't miss that part. God's people hadn't moved. They were still in the same location. The place where they'd been without water is where they would have to fight this battle.

If I were the people of Israel, I'd probably be looking for the exits. "Mo, you've got to get us out of Rephidim. There's something wrong with this place!"

Have you ever experienced that? All these dehydrating, life-sapping experiences happening in the same old place?

It's the same problems at the same church.

It's the same arguments in the same house.

It's the same unfair treatment at the same job.

It's the same gossip among the same girls, the same mess with the same men.

Who doesn't want to relocate in those circumstances?

"If I can just get out of here, things will straighten up."

"If I can remove myself from these people, problem solved."

I've said that myself. Sometimes when my buddies and I get together, one of us will comment, "If it wasn't for this one thing, everything else would be good." Yet as soon as the crazy person at work leaves for another job, the boss hires somebody who's a different kind of crazy that you have to deal with. As soon as your nosy neighbor moves out, a family full of nosys moves in.

Just like that, it was back at the bottom for the people of Israel. They were being tested a second time, in the same environment.

To make matters worse, it was Amalek. Who was he? Amalek was the grandson of Esau, who was the brother of Jacob. Jacob's name had been changed to *Israel* all those years ago. That made Amalek Jacob's great-nephew.

Yeah, that's right. Amalek was family. Someone who shared their DNA.

This time it's family standing in their way, preventing them from moving on. The kin that were supposed to be pushing Israel forward to the Promised Land were holding them back with a sword.

You know it's bad when not only can't you get help from your own bloodline but the battle is inside your house! You're walking toward your destiny, and it's family trying to stop you. It's family that's hating on you, draining you, creating drama you didn't ask for.

Matter of fact, Amalek's name meant "Man of the valley." The Israelites were having to spend time down there in the dust, dealing with him and his tribe. No way did they feel like they were at the top, breathing in that cool, fresh, mountain air. They felt like they were at the bottom. Again. The party cups gone.

God's Battle Plan

They were discovering what it's like to follow God. It's not all rainbows and sunshine. We have to go through many storms and struggles. Still, there are ways that God has called us to fight, and that's what we'll focus on in the rest of this book.

God's battle plan is in the Bible. It's important to work forward using the strategies and principles He advises so that we can ante up and face our Amaleks. We find some of those insights in Exodus 17. We will cover a few of them here and then look at more in the chapters that follow.

Keeping Perspective

After Amalek shows up, Moses commands Joshua,

> Choose men for us and go out, fight against Amalek. Tomorrow I will station myself on the top of the hill with the staff of God in my hand (verse 9).

War was about to break out. It was time for the people of Israel to fight. Joshua would take a leadership role in handling the problem down below. Meanwhile, Moses would do battle from above. Together, these two men illustrate an important truth: *The battle on the ground is won from above. So keep your eyes on the mountaintop.*

We go down to the valley to fight, knowing that God is going up the mountain to see us through the fight. Having His guidance and help is what boosts our courage to enter the battle in the first place. And it is what sustains us until the battle is won.

Connecting the spiritual, invisible realm with the physical, visible realm is a necessary part of God's battle plan. He will often call us into the canyons to do battle. Because of the kinds of struggles we face there, and the harsh environment, we can easily forget about the Lord and everything He's doing to give us victory. It really doesn't take much to convince most of us that we either have to fight alone or make a winning strategy on our own. But God says no, those are both lies. He does expect us to do our part in the midst of life's battles, but at the same time, we must never lose sight of the mountaintop because, after all, the battle is His, remember?

As my wife and I were struggling through four miscarriages, we tried the earthly approach for a while. We tried figuring things out ourselves and not really relying on God. We even got to a point where we were mad at God. Why would He put us through so much grief when our heart's desire as a couple was to "be fruitful and multiply," just like He said back in Genesis?

Eventually, though, Kanika and I came around and decided we wanted to do things God's way. We wanted to maintain a godly perspective and experience the Lord even through the hardship and the trial.

I expect that you feel the same in the battle you're fighting or else you wouldn't be reading this. In all our valleys, let's do battle God's way, as His people. That means fighting with heaven's strategies, not our own.

You've heard people say how Christians can be so heavenly minded, they're no earthly good. They're referring to the ones who do nothing but use a lot of spiritual words and walk around looking churchy. As soon as you ask them to get busy and join the battle, take on some of the earthly tasks God has given them to do, they disappear out the door. I've also seen plenty of people in the church who are so earthly minded that they're no heavenly good. These are the ones with enough confidence in their own abilities or knowledge or connections ("Hey, I know this person over here who can help me") that they leave God out. But Moses was saying, "To get this win, Joshua, you go down and I'll go up. While you deal with Amalek, I will station myself on top of the mountain with the staff of God in my hands."

Friends, we can't run from the battle when God calls us to it. We also can't successfully fight in the valley if we're not engaging spiritually. The battle is *up there*; and *up there* determines what happens down here on earth.

That's how it is with spiritual warfare. When an Amalek shows up to stop you from reaching your destiny, you can't gain the victory by ignoring heaven. As a follower of God, there's no such thing as winning battles your way. You need God's thoughts, God's methods, God's perspective, God's Word.

Winning the war involves understanding above all that the enemy we see is not the only enemy we face. Every battle must be fought in heaven and on earth, in the visible and invisible realms. They are connected. If we aren't operating in both realms at the same time, then there will be no victory. But if we hold on to heaven while taking care of earth, heaven will intervene in the here and now. We'll experience God in a whole different way.

This reminds me of a play I saw from the sidelines a few years ago during a Dallas Cowboys game. I'm the team chaplain, and one of the perks is that I get to be on the sidelines for every game. The guys always make me feel like I'm part of the team, coming over and slapping me on the head as if I have a helmet on. I sometimes have to tell them to take it easy because I'm trying to save my brain. Still, it's exciting to be so close to the action.

In this one game, the Cowboys were playing the Philadelphia Eagles, and Kyle Orton was substituting for Tony Romo at quarterback. We were on the twenty yard line, trying to score. Kyle drops back to pass and throws the ball high, into the back of the end zone. In my mind, he's throwing it away because of the defense's pressure. But I underestimated the ability of another guy on our team to get that ball.

Dez Bryant jumped for the pass, and I mean, his feet must've been forty inches off the ground. As soon as he caught the ball over his head, he immediately looked down to make sure he kept his feet inbounds. That's the way it is in the NFL—you have to have both feet on the ground and inbounds, with control of the ball up top, for the catch to count.

If Dez had had the ball in his hands but one foot out of bounds, his great catch wouldn't have mattered. If he'd had both feet inbounds but let the ball slip through his hands, play over. In order for Dez to score a touchdown, he had to have control above and below, at the same time.

That's a picture to keep with us in the valleys: Eyes on the mountaintop. Heads up. But work your feet on the ground. To win life's battles, that's what we have to do.

It's a fight to grab hold of heaven while taking care of business on earth, but it's worth it. I can imagine God saying: "Hey, if you'll look to Me as you're doing what I ask you to do down there, I will show up, and I can show off in your circumstances." That's the show we all want to see, isn't it? Where God does what only He can do, and we can celebrate with Him afterward?

The kind of opposition we're up against doesn't matter. Whether we're fighting an enemy or an obstacle, family or foe, we should be asking ourselves the mountaintop questions:

- What does God's Word say about the battle I'm facing so that I know how to execute in the valley?
- Have I prayed about what I'm going through, or am I simply complaining about what I'm going through?
- Are the people in my life speaking from the mountaintop, or do they have only an in-the-valley perspective?

Many of us don't realize that our lack of victory in the valley has everything to do with the fact that the perspective from above was never even a consideration. Exodus 17:8-13 shows us how important it is to follow our chain of command as God's people. His way, as it's communicated in His Word and through His Spirit, is our main authority within the battle. What else can we depend on? Not the world's ways. Not our own knowledge. And certainly not our feelings. Once you let your feelings define what you're facing, you'll get a double negative—the battle *and* bad feelings. (That's a valley if ever there was one!) Like a dead car battery, you have to find the positive before you can access the power to get where you're going. Every Christian's positive, every Christian's power-perspective, must be God's Word and His way, guiding you from the mountaintop.

Obedient in Battle

Exodus 17:9 is the first time Joshua is mentioned in Scripture, and his first call is to lead God's people into the valley. This is interesting because, if you flip ahead to Joshua 1, you'll see that his last call from God was to lead the people to the Promised Land.

When we get to Joshua 1, it's time—he's ready to step into his destiny as Moses's successor. But he doesn't start that way. In Exodus 17, Joshua is sent to the valley.

God will often start you low to prepare you for your promise. If He does, remember: He's not trying to down you; He's trying to raise you. Our starting place is what He uses to prepare us for our pinnacle.

Moses (and the Lord) must have seen something that told them Joshua was battle-ready. If you're in a battle, know that God sees something in you. And understand that He has either allowed it or called you to it with the intent to propel you through it. That's the perspective you and I need when we're commanded to fight. God is looking to propel us and promote us. But to do it, He may send us into the valley first.

The beginning of verse 10 says that "Joshua did just as Moses told him, and fought against Amalek." Don't skip this. Joshua was obedient. He obeyed the call of his leader to go down and take care of his responsibilities.

Joshua's obedience in the time of battle is what made him a trustworthy candidate for the time of promise. His response indicated to God and to Moses, "This is the brother for the promise."

Who doesn't want the promise? I do as much as you do! But if you want the promise, you have to be obedient in your battles. You have to prove trustworthy when Amalek comes calling. We all want it the other way: to just be trustworthy when it's easy. People are all about the blessing—"but don't give me the battle!"

Obedience in the valley is as tough as it comes. Yet Joshua's willingness to do as commanded proved that he could be relied on as Moses's successor (Joshua 1). God's servants are obedient above and below. The Lord knows who He can count on because they're as obedient in wartime as they are in peacetime. They seek Him in the battle as much as in the blessing.

Never Alone

We don't own the battle, and therefore we never have to go it alone. Ever. God supplies us in countless ways while we're in the valley. Here are three:

1. You have the power of heaven. Moses told Joshua: "It won't just be you fighting in the valley. Tomorrow, while you're battling below, I'll be up the mountain with the staff of God in my hands."

Now watch this. Though Joshua was ready for battle, it was more than he could bear on his own. Did you get that? *The battle was more than he could bear on his own.*

I know what we say to each other in the church: "Oh, God won't give you more than you can bear." Not to burst your bubble or anything, but to claim that He will only give you a weight you can carry is not biblical. The theologians among us are probably shaking their heads right now, saying, "Wait a minute, Jonathan. First Corinthians 10:13 says, 'God won't let you be tested beyond what you can bear.' What about that?"

Well, actually, it says, "God will not let you be tempted beyond what you can bear" (NIV). That verse is referring to temptation, not trials. Here, we're talking about Amalek. Amalek is not a temptation; he is a battle. Amalek represents any type of evil or enemy that shows up in your life to keep you from your destiny. While God provides a way of escape in *temptation*, we see in the lives of Job and others that sometimes our *trials* will be beyond bearing. Temptations and trials are different.

I'm sure I've messed some of you up with this. You're reading these words and worrying, *I may have to get my tattoo removed!*

You can keep the tattoo quoting 1 Corinthians 10:13. Just understand that, in times of trial, God will sometimes allow you to experience more than your load limit because that's when you recognize your need for Him. You can't know how much you need

God unless you go through some things that you definitely can't bear alone.

One time when my son Kamden was two years old, I saw him standing at the top of the stairs in our house, planning to come down all on his own. This is my strong-willed son. He wanted no help. So I tried to persuade him first: "Kamden, give me your hand, man. You don't need to be trying to do these stairs. Your legs are too short. Hold my hand or you'll look like a bowling ball coming down!"

He wouldn't take my hand, so I went up to him and grabbed his, and right then he started in—"*Na, ah, ah, ah, ah, ah!*"—real adamant that he didn't want any help. I'm pulling on him, and he's resisting me all the way. I fight him down one step, then another, drawing him up, only for him to pull me lower. We went on like this for several steps, then finally I said, "Okay, Kamden, here's your shot"…and I let him go.

He pulled his back foot off the next step before his front foot touched the ground, and *boom*! Kamden landed on his chest. This knocked the wind out of him for a second, but then it began—a toddler's worship service: Hands lifted! Crying! And coming back to the father because he recognized how foolish he was!

Now, for all you social workers, first of all, I'm outside the statute of limitations—Kamden's eight now, and healthy as can be. Second, I actually didn't let him go until the last step because I didn't want him to fall too far.

But that was the day my son started to understand, "It's just not smart to try to take this journey down here without having a hold on my father up there."

I've tried it. Doesn't work.

We have to have a strong hold on the One who is our Strength.

Two years later, Kamden was still wanting me to help him down the stairs. I would say, "You're four now, man—you take the stairs by yourself." But he'd say, "*Nunh-uh*, Daddy. Hold my hand." He knew better now.

Trying to handle what's going on in your life without having a hold of the Father, doesn't work. We ought to know better by now, right? Moses's words are that reminder to look for and ask for the help you need. Confidence in your Father gives you confidence in your fight.

Clear and simple, we only win with heaven helping us. To battle in the valley with the staff of God held on high means relying on the might of heaven to strengthen you for your earthly Amalek.

2. You have the power of community. In Exodus 17:10, we read that Moses and Joshua didn't just rely on strength from above during the battle. Joshua had an army in the valley, and Moses took Aaron and Hur with him to the top of the hill. (Aaron was Moses's brother, and Hur was apparently a trusted friend.)

Those are wise men right there, knowing they'd better take some brothers with them.

We all would think to bring others with us into a war, but to bring some support with us up the mountain is another story. For Moses, though, this was critical. Why? Because holding up the spiritual perspective is tiring.

Don't act like it isn't! Trying to be godly while a coworker is getting on your nerves for the tenth time this week will wear you out. Waiting on God to provide when the bills are due will wear you out. Trying to stay upbeat in a marriage that is breaking down will wear you out. That's why we have the body of Christ, the church. You don't—and can't—do spiritual or physical battle by yourself.

Moses couldn't, and neither can we. Verse 11 explains:

So it came about, when Moses held his hand up, that

Israel prevailed; but when he let his hand down, Amalek prevailed.

"Everything visible and physical is preceded by something invisible and spiritual." That's how my dad says it. When Moses lifted
up his hands in the spiritual realm, Israel would gain the edge in the
battle below. When God's servant lowered his hands, the enemy
would start to overcome Joshua and his men.

If you think about it, that describes us too. We get beat up a lot
of times simply because we've let our guard down spiritually. Each
of us, though, can decide, "Enough is enough. I'm going to raise my
staff and keep it raised because the spiritual realm is where the power
comes from. The spiritual realm is where I'm getting the power to
handle what I'm going through in the physical realm."

Holding up the staff is also your war cry. It shouts to everyone
around you, "I trust in the Lord. Through Him, I will prevail."

The People with You

Who are the people you want with you? Those who operate from
the same Book, who have the same perspective, who are facing the
same battle, and who want the same outcome. Those are the ones
who will have your back.

The body of Christ is so important. I don't know if I heard this in
a movie or someplace else, but you can't strike as strong a blow with
an open hand as you can with all your fingers closed tight in a fist.
Maybe that's why Hebrews 10:25 tells us to not forsake the assem-
bling of the saints. Because together, in union with other believers,
we strike a mightier blow to the enemies we face.

This is also why we have areas of connection in our churches.
If you feel like you're alone, find some friends within your faith
community. There is spiritual power—legitimate, supernatural

firepower—when God's people band together. So get into a small group. Join a Bible study. Serve in a ministry and get to know fellow believers who are moving in the same direction and using the same Playbook as you.

Trying to do it by yourself—the enemy loves that. He loves to catch you in isolation. Satan didn't attack Jesus until He was alone in the wilderness (Matthew 4). When the enemy sees you by yourself, he considers that an opportunity to jump you in hopes of bringing you down.

I often have to talk to men about this specifically, and remind myself too, because I see this as one of our biggest problems. Men, stop trying to hold the spiritual perspective without any help. We can't! I mean, I can't. I have a group of guys in my life that I call on: Keith, Marvin, Maurice, Tré, Tony, Delario, Courtney, and others.

Face it. You *will* get weary. You *will* want to get up…and give up. You *will* want to stop walking toward the destiny God has for you because these Amalekites, they're no joke. They are trying to take you out. You need some guys like Aaron and Hur riding with you. Guys you can call consistently to say, "I need you to be a witness to my life, because I'm so easily entangled by sin."

Proverbs 27:17 is clear that "as iron sharpens iron, so one person sharpens another." Galatians 6:1 says we ought to "bear one another's burdens." You've heard those verses over and over. You've got the Bible, and all these brothers and sisters around you, but you're still standing off by yourself. You can't win the battle alone. Don't enter any battle without your Aaron and your Hur.

During my mom's illness, my family knew we weren't going into the valley by ourselves. That had a big impact on our game. I want you to know that you're not fighting alone either (at least, you don't have to). The church is made up of God's people. Like the Israelites in the wilderness, we are a nation of people who band together and team up for victory.

3. *You have the power of spiritual perspective.* What was happening in the valley in Exodus 17 was determined by what was happening on the mountain. The valley didn't lead the way; the mountain did.

We live in the physical realm, but—my dad told me this—"if all you see is what you see, then you do not see all there is to be seen." Doesn't that sound like a Tony Evans statement? "If all you see is what you see, then you do not see all there is to be seen."

If you're only battling in the physical realm, without a spiritual perspective, then you may be battling in the right place...but you're not operating *from* the right place. We have to learn to operate from the top, because the text says that when Moses held up the staff, Joshua gained victory in the valley.

In that hotel room on the day my parents broke the news to us kids about my mom's cancer, Mom was sitting there taking in everyone's reaction, and the first words out of her mouth were Scripture, a paraphrase of Ephesians 6:12: "Y'all know that this fight is not against flesh and blood. This fight is against the principalities and powers and forces of darkness that war in heavenly places. The enemy is attacking, so we need to fight."

Many of you are dealing with health issues. You're dealing with financial issues. You're dealing with relational or parenting issues, or addiction issues. Regardless of the battle you're in, it's a spiritual battle above all. There are things going on in the supernatural realm—forces beyond what your eyes can see—that are actively working to defeat you, even destroy you. The battle is your opportunity to pull down the power of heaven to overcome what's coming at you on earth.

The call has to come from the top, and then it gets executed at the bottom. This is what I learned from playing football my whole life.

During the game, a team's offensive coordinators will sit up in the box and call plays down to the field. The job of the top is to call the plays for the bottom. The job of the bottom is to execute the plays called from the top. If there's nobody at the top calling plays, it doesn't matter how skillful the players are; their skill alone can't defeat the opposition. The ones who win are the ones who get their plays from above.

When we recognize that every earthly battle is part of the spiritual war, it changes our perspective. We let the Lord have the lead. We let God decide the battle plan and guide us to victory. And we never have to back down.

With Him in charge, we can take over situations that would like to overtake us. With Him in charge, we can overcome what tries to come over us.

Victorious

Though Moses was being obedient in the battle, his hands got "heavy." So what did Aaron and Hur do? Pay attention to this now—this is a beast! Aaron and Hur "took a stone and put it under him, and he sat on it" (verse 12). You know you have the right people around you when they give you a stone to rest on when you get tired.

But I see more than that here. It's like Aaron and Hur were saying, "In this battle, we can't have Joshua out there getting whupped. We need to sit you on the rock, Moses, so that you can keep holding up the spiritual staff when it gets heavy."

Aaron and Hur gave Moses something strong to rest on: They put God's Word beneath him.

When the battle makes you tired, godly companions won't give you what you want to hear—they'll give you what you need to hear. They're going to keep sliding that rock under you.

"Oh, you're tired? Sit on this."

"You're worn out from holding up a godly perspective? Let's pray together."

"You're tired of going to church? You can sit in the passenger seat—you don't even have to drive."

Fighting battles God's way means that we will sit and rest on the rock of God's Word. As your brother in the Lord, I'm not going to give you my opinion, or what my parents told me; I'm going to give you what *God* says. This is one way I can help you stay strong until the battle is won.

We have to have brothers and sisters who can support us, pray for us, surround us, and speak the truth to us so that the truth can set us free. That's exactly what Moses's helpers did: "Aaron and Hur supported [Moses's] hands, one on one side and one on the other. So his hands were steady until the sun set" (verse 12).

Finally, the passage says in verse 13 that "Joshua defeated Amalek and his people with the edge of the sword." Because Moses's hands were steady in the spiritual realm, Joshua overwhelmed the enemy in the physical realm.

I love that, don't you? There was victory in the valley because the spiritual battle was won on the mountaintop.

The battle on the field in front of us is never the only story. We experience victory or defeat here on earth based on what's happening upstairs, in the spiritual realm. You may be in the valley, and it may look like you're losing, but keep watching for what God is doing up top while you're handling your assignment on the ground. Keep letting Him call the plays for you. This is what puts you in position to win.

I'm telling you, if we can learn to look to God spiritually, we can have victory physically.

If we can learn to value the eternal, we can have victory even now.

If we can learn to obey in the hard times, joining forces with faithful people by our side, then we can overcome Amalek with our sword. We can go to war and win because we take the staff of God—the Word of God, the power of God—with us.

Never lose sight of the mountaintop, friend. And don't quit on your earthly responsibilities either. Even though it's difficult…be faithful in your marriage. Do your work well. Keep your promises to your kids. And take care of your relationships and your finances and your commitments. Then you'll see God come through like He came through for Joshua, Moses, and ultimately the people of Israel.

My mom looked to God during her battle with cancer, *and* she acted responsibly. She went to the doctor. Followed medical protocol. Went on a strict diet with all the sugars removed (because sugar feeds cancer cells). She fought *and* she believed God's Word. She did, and we did as a family.

And we won.

How did we win, you ask? I mean, my mom did die of cancer after a great fight.

Well, if we could hear her now, I'm sure she would say, "I won big. If only you could see what I see."

You may not win the way you think you will, or the way you pray to win. But God has victory in store for those who trust Him.

"This is not a time to tuck tail and run." That's something else my mom said on that sad day. This is not a time to let your guard down in either realm. Go be responsible and fight hard. Keep your eye on the mountaintop, because what happens up there determines your overwhelming victory down here.

The doctors may give you a bad diagnosis. Your workplace may give you bad news. Your own family may be fighting you as you seek to follow the Lord. In every situation you can say, "My eyes are on You, Lord," because both the valley and the victory are in His hands.

Scan the QR code or visit
https://jonathanblakeevans.com/fyb-film-1/
to view a message from Jonathan.
(chapters 1–3)

CHAPTER 4

KEEP IT CLOSE

One objective of God's plan for fighting our battles is: Never forsake the spiritual perspective as you do your daily business. We saw that in the previous chapter. Life happens in two realms at the same time—in heaven and on earth. They are so interconnected that your efforts on the ground will ultimately fail unless you're getting your plays from above. You need to complete your assignments on the field while you consult your Coach. Then you can keep advancing toward the promises God has for you.

When we grab hold of heaven and its perspective, we are also grabbing hold of God's Word as our battle plan. It's essential for taking care of our earthly responsibilities and overcoming the enemy's efforts.

The World and the Word

We have to keep God's Word close to maintain the spiritual perspective in the midst of our battles. We also need it to continue moving forward in the midst of the daily grind.

I've had times where I thought I could reach for the world for some situations and reach for the Word for others. I've tried using the world's playbook to win some games and God's Playbook to win others. But this creates a dangerous imbalance.

To try to grab on to both the Word and the world is like weightlifting with dumbbells. You can't hold those separate weights in balance for long. They'll put you off-kilter, where you're favoring one side over the other. And as weight is added to both your left and your right hand, you'll eventually drop the worldly dumbbell because that's always the weak side. The straight bar of God's Word keeps you in balance. It won't throw off your form. His truth on both sides of you, held together by the iron of His character—that's what gives you stability.

Not only does God's Word stabilize us for our battles but it endures. It never needs updating. It's powerful and effective for every play of every season for your entire life. His Word holds up in the worst scenarios. Against the toughest opponents. And on every kind of playing field. In 2 Timothy 3:16-17, we're reminded that because Scripture has been given to us by God—who never changes—it is constantly "useful." With it, He prepares and equips His people "to do every good work" (NLT), teaching us what is true and right, and correcting us when we are wrong.

The world, though, operates the opposite. It's constantly revising its playbook. People add pages, throw out old plays, and experiment with other methods all the time, hoping to find some new strategy for success. So one day we're told, "The latest studies show that you should trust your heart!" Another day, some motivational speaker pops up and says, "Read my book!" The next day, we're advised to explore our talents or work our connections if we want to win.

Excuse me? Let's get it right, right out of the gate: We need a word from the Lord *at all times*. We need His Word for every play on the field and every battle of our lives, not the cultural strategies that we hear about every day.

It's the difference between building on rock or sand.

In Luke 6, Jesus talked about two guys building houses. One man chose rock for his foundation, and the other chose sand. Then along comes a storm. By the time the storm has passed, the man who built his house on sand is homeless, while the man who built his house on a rock, his house still stands. The difference was in what the house was resting on.

Now, what's the difference between rock and sand?

Sand is the world. Rock is God's Word.

Sand is human opinion. Rock is God's revelation.

Sand is what people think. Rock is what God thinks.

A lot of Christians try to mix rock and sand. They want God's opinion mixed with human opinion. They go to church and hear the Word on Sunday, but then they go to work on Monday and want to hear what everybody else thinks.

Our problem is that many of us are getting fluff from the people we hang out with. Their strategies have nothing to do with what God says. And then we wonder why our trials and tribulations are beating us down.

God is saying, *Trust Me. Read My Book. Connect with Me!* There's no sense in waiting until every worldly strategy fails before reaching for your Bible. You shouldn't have to have the pressure turned up in your life before saying, "I need a word from the Lord." His Word is not our last resort!

His Word can fight for you in your battles and be your joy within the daily grind. But you have to keep it close by *taking up* God's Word and *taking in* God's Word as though your life depends on it. Which it does. The minute you drop your guard and decide you can skip either of these practices, you're only making yourself an open target. You're entering the battle empty handed and entering the game of life without a game plan.

Whether you're going out to do battle or you're going out to do life, we have to have this truth ironclad in our minds: the Word of God not only shows us how to live and how to fight, but it is *what we live by and fight back with.*

Moses learned this from experience. He encountered so many scenarios in his journey with God that even when something unprecedented happened, he knew what to do. He just knew.

Numbers 21 tells us there was a time when Moses had to lift up a bronze serpent on a pole in order for the Israelites to be saved from death. Because the people had spoken out against Him, God sent serpents among them, and many men and women and children died from snake bites. Israel confessed, and God provided a way of escape, instructing Moses to make a bronze serpent and lift it up on a pole. Anyone who laid eyes on it would be saved if they'd been bitten.

That's one way to think about our battles. We're in some venomous valley situations, surrounded by poisonous snakes. But by looking to God—by casting our eyes on the Lord and making His holiness and righteousness our standard for handling the situations we face—we'll soon see how biblical truth saves us.

Take It Up

Exodus 17:13 sums up the battle against Amalek succinctly: "Joshua defeated Amalek and his people with the edge of the sword." Joshua won with what? *The edge of the sword.* What is the sword? The Word of God. Ephesians 6 says that.

Looking at the "full armor" of God as it's detailed there, we see that it includes the helmet of salvation, the breastplate of righteousness, the belt of truth, the shoes of peace, and the shield of faith (verses 13-17). All those things are defensive mechanisms. In other words, they stop you from getting wounded. But they don't fight back.

The sword is important because it's the only offensive weapon you get. The one thing you can use in your battle to overwhelm your enemy and send him running is the sword of truth.

Hear me on this. There's nothing wrong with putting up a good defense. Our armor is from the Lord, just like our ability to avoid sin and flee the devil. The problem is, too many of us are *only* playing defense. But the Bible says we can take our game both ways. We can actually go on the offensive too—praying with expectation, obeying with expectation—confident that, even though we have battles, God is preparing us for a great promise:

- "If you remain in Me and My words remain in you, ask whatever you wish, and it will be done for you" (John 15:7).

- "Your word is a lamp to my feet and a light to my path" (Psalm 119:105).

- "Prove yourselves doers of the word, and not just hearers who deceive themselves…One who has looked intently at the perfect law, the law of freedom, and has continued in it, not having become a forgetful hearer but an active doer, this person will be blessed in what he does" (James 1:22,25).

- "Blessed is the one who reads, and those who hear the words of the prophecy and keep the things which are written in it; for the time is near" (Revelation 1:3).

The Lord told Joshua specifically, "This Book of the Law shall not depart from your mouth, but you shall meditate on it day and night, so that you may be careful to do according to all that is written in it; for then you will make your way prosperous, and then you will achieve success" (Joshua 1:8). He is saying the same to you and to me: "Don't drop the Book! Don't let it depart from you. Don't ignore it. If you want to win this war, you'd better know My Word."

God said it, so we're going to do it. We're going to take up the sword of the Lord and use it. Rely on it. Trust what it says.

To not know God's Word means you can be hustling and handling your responsibilities here on earth—and life can still tear you up because you aren't brandishing a weapon. Hustle alone won't protect you. A warrior needs his or her sword. Take up God's Word and use it on the battlefield, and you will prevail. Leave it sitting on the shelf at home, all nice and shiny, and you will suffer great defeat.

With that being true, why don't we know the Bible? Why don't we?

We treat it like something we can set aside while we live life, as if it gets in our way. Why? Why isn't it a daily essential? Why do we let life go flat before we lay hold of it? We pull the Bible out of the trunk of our lives like it's a spare tire. And then, once we're rolling again, we put it back in the trunk until we hit the next pothole.

This practice of ours reminds me of Paul's plea about another practice he was seeing among fellow believers. He told them: "My brothers and sisters, this should not be" (James 3:10 NIV).

Maybe you aren't fighting back in your battle right now because you've dropped the sword. But the Bible is what gets you through the battle so that you can make it to the promise.

Keep your guard up, and don't get lazy. Take up the sword God has given you.

I can tell you right now, you're not going to want to do that when your emotions are running strong. The most difficult thing in life is to obey the Word of God in the heat of battle, when you're all in your feelings. Life's trials and tribulations will make you want to discard biblical truth for something that feels good, seems easier, or offers a quick fix.

You know that challenge as well as I do. You've faced it in some capacity.

How hard it is to be biblical when your spouse is going astray. Or when your supervisor is disrespecting you or your coworker is undermining you. How hard it is to choose righteousness when your grown children are making crazy choices or your family is pushing all your buttons.

Yes, it's a battle. But we must believe that God's Word will give us the wisdom and the strength to fight and win. God calls us to fight in His Word. He calls us to win through His Word. His calling us means He will strengthen us.

Don't let the heart of your inner man pull you from the heart of God and His Word. If the sword is the Word of God, and Joshua overwhelmed Amalek with the edge of the sword, you know what you need to do to overwhelm your Amaleks. You have to pick up your sword.

God's Word should never be forsaken in times of battle. In order to turn back the opponents you face, it's going to take the sword. God's sword.

Take It In

A second strategy for keeping our guard up is to *take in* the Word. Let me share a biblical scene to help illustrate what I mean.

The first several verses of 2 Samuel 6 tell us that David, as king of Israel, was intent on bringing the ark of God back to Jerusalem. The book of 1 Samuel gives us the historical background. "The Philistines fought and Israel was defeated, and every man fled to his tent; and the defeat was very great, for thirty thousand foot soldiers of Israel fell. Moreover, the ark of God was taken." That's recorded in 4:10-11. Then, 7:1-2 reports,

> The men of Kiriath-jearim came and took the ark of the Lord and brought it into the house of Abinadab on the hill, and they consecrated his son Eleazar to watch over the ark of the Lord. From the day that the ark remained at Kiriath-jearim, the time was long, for it was twenty years; and all the house of Israel mourned after the Lord.

The ark of the Lord, also known as the ark of the covenant or the ark of God, was a gold chest with two angel-like figures (cherubim) at the top that were also made of gold. Inside this pure-gold chest were the two stone tablets on which Moses had carved the Ten Commandments given to him by the Lord:

> "Thou shalt have no other gods before me."

> "Thou shalt not make unto thee any graven image."

> "Thou shalt not take the name of the LORD thy God in vain."

> "Remember the sabbath day, to keep it holy."

> "Honour thy father and thy mother."

> "Thou shalt not kill."

> "Thou shalt not commit adultery."

> "Thou shalt not steal."

> "Thou shalt not bear false witness against thy neighbour."

> "Thou shalt not covet thy neighbour's house…nor anything that is thy neighbour's."

> (Exodus 20 KJV)

To bring the ark back to Jerusalem, "David again gathered all the chosen men of Israel, thirty thousand. And David departed from Baale-judah, with all the people who were with him, to bring up from there the ark of God." As the ark was being carried home to Jerusalem, "David and all the house of Israel were celebrating before the LORD with all kinds of instruments made of juniper wood, and with lyres, harps, tambourines, castanets, and cymbals" (2 Samuel 6:1-2,5-6).

It was a big deal, worthy of a huge party. The ark had been absent from the holy city for twenty years! On the return, though, they ran into some trouble. The ark nearly overturned when the oxen stumbled. Uzzah, one of the men accompanying the ark, grabbed on to it. "And the anger of the LORD burned against Uzzah, and God struck him down there for his irreverence" (verses 6-7).

This can be a tough passage to understand. Why would God strike Uzzah down for trying to keep the ark upright? I think it's because the ark (which represents God's commands, His word to His people) isn't just something you can have good intentions toward. Obedience is God's requirement.

He had warned all of Israel: "After Aaron and his sons have finished covering the holy furnishings and all the holy articles, and when the camp is ready to move, only then are the Kohathites to come and do the carrying. But they must not touch the holy things or they will die. The Kohathites are to carry those things that are in the tent of meeting" (Numbers 4:15 NIV). The ark of the Lord was one of those sacred items.

Anytime we stumble in life, we're going to have a reflex response, but is that reflex obedient or disobedient? Is our natural response the biblical response? If not, we have to change because the Word of God will always remain the same.

People hold up the Word in the wrong ways all the time. They pick the parts they like and skip the parts they don't. Or they turn it into legalism and judgment, and beat "sinners" over the head with it like the Pharisees did. And we probably all know at least one person who has mishandled Scripture by misinterpreting or misapplying it. Somebody may have good intentions initially, but good intentions don't always translate into godly obedience. His Word is extremely important. It has to be obeyed.

As soon as God struck Uzzah dead, that display of holy anger convinced David to call off the procession and cancel the party. Not wanting to risk angering the Lord any further, Israel's king commanded that the ark be left in the home of a man named Obed-edom.

Three months later, David received a status report: "The LORD has blessed the house of Obed-edom and all that belongs to him, on account of the ark of God." This told David that God was no longer angry. "So David went and brought the ark of God up from the house of Obed-edom to the city of David with joy…And David was dancing before the LORD with all his strength" (2 Samuel 6:12,14). Verse 16 adds that as the ark entered Jerusalem, David—King David—was out there "leaping and dancing before the LORD."

Can you see it? The Hebrew says he was "whirling." I mean, he was going crazy in the streets in front of all the people.

Why did this matter so much? What difference did it make to have this sacred container in Jerusalem? The Commandments in the chest signified God's covenant with His people. The Lord had said, "If you follow these laws, your days will be prolonged. I will go with you, and you will multiply greatly in the land. If you follow these covenants, I will take care of your families. If you follow these regulations, you will experience freedom. You will experience joy."

The words in the chest equaled a blessing. Are you with me?

David was leaping and whirling around and rejoicing because the ark of God meant the presence of God was with His people. And with His presence comes His blessing.

David understood that the governing guidelines God had put in place meant that he could experience blessing and joy as a king and also pass these good things along to his people. We see it in verses 17-19. Once the ark of the Lord was set in its place in the tabernacle where God's people worshiped, "David offered burnt offerings and peace offerings before the Lord. When David had finished offering the burnt offering and peace offerings, he blessed the people in the name of the Lord of armies." He also sent every household home with bread and drink and meat.

The Word in the chest represented the presence of God, and the presence of God meant a blessing on the people. Then and now, the Word of God blesses those who obey it.

Hundreds of years after David, Jesus verified this, saying to all who would follow Him, "Blessed are those who hear the word of God and follow it" (Luke 11:28). "If you continue in My word, then you are truly My disciples; and you will know the truth, and the truth will set you free" (John 8:31-32). "These things I have spoken to you so that My joy may be in you, and that your joy may be made full" (John 15:11).

God's words in that golden chest meant everything. They still do. But you don't have to carry around a golden chest if you will commit to having the Word of God living in your chest. If it's *in* you, the power, presence, and purpose of God is automatically *with* you.

A Book of Joy and Freedom

Most people think the Bible is a book of restrictions and rules. I see it as a book of joy and freedom. That's why it has rules in it. Not to restrict us but to free us.

In Deuteronomy 6:20 the question is asked, Why should we obey God's commands? "What do these things mean?"

God answers in entire chapters, not just verses! *My commands are for your good and your survival, your joy and your blessing.*

In effect, God is trying to save your life with His Word. He saves His people from sin, and by obeying His instructions, they are also saved from the enemy's lies and the foolishness of the world. If we have His Word, we have His presence in us and with us, all the way to heaven.

The Lord's commands protect us, free us, and bring us joy.

Protection. Without His commands, we get caught in situations that we can't get ourselves out of.

I raised pit bulls in college. Not the biting ones! I had sweet-tempered, beautiful, show-dog pit bulls. I set up a kennel in my backyard, bred my dogs, and sold the puppies. That's how I made money back then.

To ship my first dog, Deuce, from California my sophomore year cost me fifteen hundred dollars. He was a big dude, about eighty-five pounds. And he was pretty, with a blue-and-white coat and a big head. It was huge—twenty-four inches! One of the things I love about pit bulls is the size of their heads.

I set up my entire backyard for Deuce and his pack. And I paid a hefty price for him to be safe. I mean, I built a six-foot fence out there. I had toys for him, his food and water, and of course, a female. I married those two dogs so that I could have puppies biblically.

Deuce had everything he needed, and with that six-foot fence, I wasn't worried about him getting out. But one day Deuce tried his best. He kept running back and forth, looking through the fence and wagging his tail. I knew he was wanting to get to something that was beyond the fence, but I figured there wasn't any way, so I went inside. Deuce, though, really wanted to get out. So he started digging. Since he couldn't jump the fence, he tried to dig under it, thinking he could manufacture his own freedom. Once he thought he had dug deep enough, he took his shot. Burrowed into the hole. Only problem was, he didn't consider the size of his head.

Those twenty-four inches got in his way. His head got stuck between the ground and the fence, and as soon as he got hung up, he started yelping. I rushed out there, and at first I was heated. And because I'm not God—I'm a decent master, but I'm not a perfect master—I mocked Deuce. "Yeah, that's what you get for trying to leave my yard. Your head is big. You should've stayed where you are!" I said it out loud because I wanted to make sure that Maya, the female dog, heard me so that she wouldn't try it. Of course they couldn't understand what I was saying, but it made me feel better.

I did cool off a little once I saw how stuck he was. He was so wedged in that I actually had to inflict more pain on him to get him out of his mess. I had to press his head to the ground to create a gap for him to back up, back into my yard.

Deuce didn't get what he thought he wanted. But the pain I inflicted on him at least brought him back to my presence. Brought him back to the place where he was protected and completely cared for.

A lot of people do like Deuce: they try to make their own way as if they know better than the Master. Sure enough, their big heads get them stuck in a situation they can't get out of. Then what do they do? They react. They become reactive because they weren't proactive about staying in their Master's yard. The price that Christ has paid to protect them and give them a victorious, thriving life isn't enough. They're looking for something beyond the yard.

God sometimes has to inflict more pain to get us in a position where we say, "You know what? I think I'll stay right here. I'm a whole lot safer inside the boundaries of this yard that He has set up."

We are already living inside the boundaries of His sovereignty. We are already cared for in every way, and we are safe. Nothing beyond His fence is anything we need.

Freedom. I often hear people define freedom as "being able to do whatever I want to do, whenever I want to do it." That's not freedom. That's chaos. If players could run anywhere in the stadium for a touchdown, nobody would win. In fact, everybody loses because a touchdown would mean nothing.

Do you want to dance in the locker room? Have the taste of victory? Then you have to have rules on the field. Too many penalty flags and you won't get the win that you're after. But play within the rules, and you're free to score. The boundaries actually let you play the game the way it's meant to be played.

Joy. As we've seen, with the presence of God comes the promise of God, His blessing. He gives it to you—you don't have to manufacture or find your happiness. He also makes it full, to overflowing. Hebrews 12:10-11 reminds us that God's discipline (His limitations on us) is "for our good, in order that we may share in his holiness" and produce "a harvest of righteousness and peace" (NIV). A harvest is more than we can possibly enjoy in one sitting. A harvest means blessings multiplied—blessings to enjoy and to share—not just today but for many days, months, or years ahead.

We sometimes like to create our own happy scenarios. The problem is, they don't last very long. Happiness is fleeting because it is always based on *what's happening.* Joy is very different. The joy that comes with this Word made David dance. It made David, a very rich king, say over and over in the psalms, "Nothing is better than the law of God!" That sounds like full-on joy to me.

The Recipe

Every member of God's family needs to take this Word and put it in their chest. You and I need to marinate in the Word—soak it in and soak it up—because God's rules and regulations are the recipe for actual joy.

I sometimes reminisce on how good a cook my mom was. Listen, when we'd get to the holidays each year, it went down. Talk about macaroni and cheese—I loved her macaroni and cheese! I don't know what all she put in it, but once that bubbly goodness came out of the oven and she set it on the table, my holidays were made.

She'd call out, "Jon Jon, you ready?" And I'd go in the dining room and put my hand out. She'd hand me a fork and I'd walk up to the dish. Taste-test time! Then I'd just start dancing. You know how, when food is good, you dance over it? While you're eating it?

My siblings would follow me to the table, and they'd be like, "Oh, Jon Jon has his macaroni and cheese!" And they'd each grab a fork, and we'd all be in a line, dancing over that macaroni and cheese, all four of us.

Those memories stand out even more because I can remember trying to self-manufacture my mom's macaroni and cheese one time in college. I didn't worry about getting her recipe. I figured, *I've eaten it long enough to try to do it on my own.* So I made a batch, and it kind of looked like Mom's as I took it out of the oven.

I couldn't wait to have some. I took a scoop, blew on it, put it in my mouth...and I spit that mess out as soon as it went in.

Time to call the expert and confess: "Mom, I messed up. What did I do wrong? I put this in there, and this, and I added some of that."

She laughed. "Boy, you forgot the cheese!"

Now, before you start judging me, my mom used several different kinds of cheese in her recipe. I forgot a couple of them. But the scenario comes to mind because that time, even though I had the expectation of joy, I couldn't dance because I tried to do things my way. I didn't stick to the recipe.

You may want to tell me about the restriction of the recipe: "Oh, a recipe limits you." But I'll tell you about the precision of the taste: "Following the recipe makes it taste so good!" That's probably why the Bible tells us:

> Taste and see that the LORD is good;
> How blessed is the man who takes refuge in Him!
> (Psalm 34:8).

The Difference Between Victory and Defeat

By his example and his words, David was saying, "People, you need to get this Word in your chest." How do you do that practically?

It starts with *reading and hearing the Word*. Find a good, Bible-teaching church so you can hear the Word and learn to read it for all it's worth. That church may not be the biggest one in your city. It may not be the one with all the billboards or the flashy sign out front. It may not be the church that your friends consider cool. What matters is, are those believers seeking God and teaching His Word, or are they soothing themselves with a nice little verse here and there?

Reading and hearing the Word isn't the only way you put it in your chest. You know how else you do it? You *apply it*. Sitting in a meeting room listening to a coach talk about the *X*s and *O*s isn't what teaches players how to react within the game. The reason the best players can react instantly, as if it's second nature, is because they're practicing those instructions every single day, and then they take all that experience with them out on the field.

Until you practice the Word, it will stay on the surface; it won't get inside you. Until you practice applying it, you're not really ready to take the field.

I know Christians who are game-day analysts, don't you? They like to watch from the sidelines, but don't ask them to suit up and get in the game. They're content to come to church, listen to Pastor So-and-So, and then hurry out the door right after the service and spend their lunchtime commenting on how good or bad the message was.

What are we doing? We have wars to win and battles to fight! People around us are sick. They're losing loved ones. They have wayward children. Their marriages are falling apart. They're losing their jobs and surrendering to addictions. God has called us to hear and do His Word, not to just sit around and analyze it. He wants us ministering to others, caring for others, fulfilling His commands, and sharing His Word.

The victory comes, the blessing comes, through His Word in your chest. And that comes from application—from acting on what you've learned. James 1:22 says, "Prove yourselves doers of the word, and not merely hearers who delude themselves" (NASB 1995). If you've ever drunk an open can of soda that's been sitting too long, you know how gross it is. It's gross because it has lost its fizz. A lot of people have lost their fizz because they hear but they don't do.

Put this Word in your chest and practice it. Put it into play so it becomes second nature. Most of all, apply His truth *in your situation*. In your comings and goings, in your relationships and conversations, as you work and play and meet and worship and serve. In everything you do in life, the Word of God makes the difference. Act on it. It is the difference between victory and defeat.

CHAPTER 5

HIGHER THAN YOU THINK

ever, never do battle without God. We need Him all the time. All. The. Time. His power is always on. He alone is your power source. But how often are you accessing Him? How often are you activating His power, where you're experiencing the connection through prayer and dependence on Him?

Your ability to face any enemy and fight any battle is only as good as your connection with Him. We see this in Joshua 7, but not in the way you might expect. Here's the context:

> Now Joshua sent men from Jericho to Ai, which is near Beth-aven, east of Bethel, and said to them, "Go up and spy out the land." So the men went up and spied out Ai. Then they returned to Joshua and said to him, "Do not have all the people go up; have only about two or three thousand men go up and attack Ai; do not trouble all the people there, for they are few" (verses 2-3).

The spies come back with their report and recommendations: "This one's easy. We don't need a lot of men to get the job done. If we take a few thousand guys in there, we can take the city." Verse 4 tells us that Joshua went along with what they said: "So about three thousand men from the people went up there…" But the verse ends with this critical piece of info: "but they fled from the men of Ai."

What? Joshua's boys had just finished saying, "That city is small. Not a big deal." So why did the men of Israel end up running from Ai?

Apparently Joshua and his advisors thought they could do battle without God. But the Israelites found out (and I want to make sure that we understand too): *It's much higher than you think.* Every battle, every calling, extends much higher than we think, involving more than what meets the eye.

Read verses 2-4 again, this time all together:

> Now Joshua sent men from Jericho to Ai, which is near Beth-aven, east of Bethel, and said to them, "Go up and spy out the land." So the men went up and spied out Ai. Then they returned to Joshua and said to him, "Do not have all the people go up; have only about two or three thousand men go up and attack Ai; do not trouble all the people there, for they are few." So about three thousand men from the people went up there, but they fled from the men of Ai.

What word do you see over and over again in this passage? *Up.*

So we're learning that Joshua miscalculated. The spies miscalculated. Even though Ai was small, it was *up.* It was beyond even Joshua's paygrade. The battle was a lot higher than any of them thought.

Most of us perceive things physically, by their size, never considering that what we see in the physical is fortified by something that's UP. In the spiritual realm. Yet this is what Ephesians 6:12 says. Our battles in this life aren't really against "flesh and blood" but "against the rulers, against the powers, against the world forces of this darkness, against the spiritual forces of wickedness in the heavenly places." That's why we need to go to God in every situation and circumstance. Because for everything we perceive in the physical realm, there is always something else—something higher—going on in the spiritual realm.

My son Kamden wanted to get to a ball that was way above his head, and so he grabbed a ladder and climbed onto it.

"Don't go up there," I told him. "It's too high."

"Dad, I can do it."

If you know how I parent, you know I said, "Alright, then, go ahead."

So Kamden gets to the top rung, and he looks down and says, "*Huh.*" Next he starts shaking. Then he says, "Dad, get me."

I said, "Nope. Come down one step at a time."

He's shaking the whole time, coming down this ladder. Shaking and shaking, step by step.

He gets to the bottom. He's breathing hard. "Dad, that was much higher than I thought!"

"I know, son."

"Next time, I should just ask you to do it."

"I know, son."

"Can you do it?"

"Sure, son."

I reached up and grabbed the ball without even getting on the ladder and gave it to Kamden. He said, "Wow, Dad, you're tall."

I said, "I know, son."

He said, "Man, that was higher than I thought. From now on, I'll just ask you to do it because you're taller than anything I need to reach on my own."

Just like Kamden, you and I have climbed high, thinking we

could stretch to reach a solution—and then realized too late that all we'd done was scare ourselves. Meanwhile, God is listening for each of His children to admit, "Oooo, that's higher than I thought, God. Can You do it for me?"

That's when your situation starts to shift. That's when you can experience Him doing "far more abundantly beyond all that we ask or think, according to the power that works within us" (Ephesians 3:20).

A Saving Environment

Let me say it again: What we see is not all there is. God is always working to bring us higher. It's just that some of us (I'm pointing at myself too) don't always let Him.

My wife, Kanika, is the penny-pincher in our family. When I say penny-pincher, I'm talking about literally *pinching the penny*. She tries not to let anything leave our house unless it's appropriately spent. I'm all for saving money, but I don't like how long it sometimes takes to shop for those savings. Especially at a place like Target.

Once Kanika walks through those doors, she pulls up this price-scanning app, and then she's *beep, beep, beep*—just scanning away all over the store. I try to help out and be a good husband, but I struggle because, after a while, I'm ready to get out of there! As if this is taking my precious time.

The first time I saw her scanning things, I asked, "What are you doing?"

"Being connected to this app gives you savings," Kanika said. "You really ought to try it."

I wasn't interested. "*Eh*, you're probably saving a nickel or a dime; it's not a big deal."

Sometimes, to try to move things along, I've even told her, "Hey, close your eyes so you don't see anything else and stop on our way to checkout." I'll be guiding her, but then she'll open one eye and veer off in that direction, *beep, beep, beep*—scanning more stuff. And I'm saying to myself, "Man, if we don't get out of this store…" I'm thinking about the time; my wife, she's thinking about *the dime!*

On one of these trips, Kanika knew by the time we finally got to the cash register that I was frustrated at all the running around. As the cashier rang up our items (*more scanning!*), my wife smiled at me, knowing what was coming.

The first item beeps. "Look, babe, we saved fifty cents!"

The next item—*beep*. "Baby, seventy-five cents!"

Beep. "Babe, we saved a dollar!" She does this all sing-songy, just to get under my skin.

So my wife is making songs, and I'm standing there feeling irritated: *This little-bitty savings that you're talking about right now, who cares? Let's go!*

Once we finally get home, Kanika tells me, "I know you think it's small, but the savings add up. I saved twenty dollars today. The week before, I saved thirty. And the week before that, it was even more."

She's talking to me, and I'm looking at her, but I'm kind of looking through her, you know? I'm not really listening because I'm still frustrated. (Wives, I know ya'll are thinking, *Yeah, that's exactly what my husband does.*) That is, until Kanika added everything up and gave me the final number. The final number after so many months of visits to the store, scanning all that stuff.

All of a sudden I zeroed back in. All of a sudden I could hear my wife again, because the number was much higher than I thought. All of a sudden, I'm saying, "Now tell me about that app! I need to download it, whatever it's called." I wanted that app because I wanted to be connected to something that could take me higher than I thought.

Joshua, it seems to me, had ignored the connection. We read about him sending up his men to do battle and take a city in Joshua 7, but one thing we don't see in this passage is God. From what I can tell, Joshua decided to move forward without seeking the Lord about this battle, even though the Lord had given him victory again and again and again, including victory in the region they were currently in.

They were near Jericho, a fortress-of-a-city where the Israelites had seen God's power in action. They had just defeated the people of Jericho by blowing trumpets and shouting, y'all! Not one Israelite laid even one finger on the walls of Jericho! Those thick, massive walls had crumbled at the hand of God. So why in the world would Joshua think he could take Ai without any help from God?

Because he perceived the fight to be a small one.

How many times do you and I move forward just like this, leaving God in our pocket? *Eh, this isn't one I need to spend a whole lot of time on or even ask people to pray about.* We keep the "God app" closed because "I've got this. I can handle it." The fight looks small enough to win by ourselves.

This teaches me a principle. It lets me know that *what I perceive has almost nothing to do with what I achieve.* I achieve by connecting. Kanika's connection with that app put us in an environment that saves, and it brought us a whole lot higher—with a much bigger impact on our budget—than I ever thought it would.

Basing our decisions on our perception alone is never a good idea. Anytime I trust what I'm seeing over what God sees and says about a problem, my eyes are going to lead me down a dead-end path. In my battles and my callings, I'm in the "ready" position only if I care less about what I see and care more about connecting with what, and especially Who, can actually save me.

No Comparison

The spies that Joshua sent to Ai came back claiming, "Shouldn't be an issue. The enemy is small." But then, don't you hate it when something you perceived as little turns into a really big issue? Before they knew it, the Israelites came back down, running from the fight, because the problem was more than they thought it would be.

If you think your battle, your enemy, your situation is small, let me ask: Small in comparison to whom? To whom are you comparing your problem?

Obviously, the spies thought more of themselves than they should have. In order to call their problem small, in order to believe that God could sit this one out, the spies had to think they were big.

In Numbers 13, most of Moses's guys made the same mistake of comparing their situation to themselves, but they drew a different conclusion. Y'all remember that story? Moses sent twelve men—including Joshua—to Canaan to spy out the people there. Joshua and Caleb came back saying, "With God's help, we can defeat them." Ten of the twelve, though, gave this report: "The enemy is too big. We are like grasshoppers in their sight. We don't stand a chance."

The people sided with those guys, and they grumbled against Moses. Long story short: Nobody ended up asking God for help. Not for help or courage. As a result, the Israelites didn't go forward and take the land that God told them to take. Their view was, *That problem is too big for us to do what God told us to do.*

In Joshua 7, their view was, *That problem is so small, we don't need God at all.*

Either way, they left God out.

Most people have pride wrong. Most people think pride is only when you think high of yourself. But pride is also when you think low of yourself. If I'm so down on myself that I don't bring God in on what He is calling me to do, then I'm just as prideful as the person who thinks they've got it covered. In both situations, I'm using myself as the determining factor. Pride shows itself anytime you make *you* the reason for leaving God on the sidelines.

A lot of us have gotten caught in that. I have gotten caught in that. I remember another story of Moses where he got caught in that too, in Exodus 3. God—who was speaking from a burning bush—called Moses to get in front of Pharaoh and say, "Let My people go." In verse 11, Moses responded, "Who am I?" *Who am I that You would send me to Pharaoh?* A few verses later, God reminded Moses, "I AM." *I am the God who provides for you.*

Notice the difference. Moses looked at himself and asked, "Am I?" *Am I really the one to do this?* And God said, "No, you're not—but I AM. I AM THAT I AM." *I'm everything that you need.*

Most of us are looking at some challenge, some battle in front of us, and we're downing ourselves: "Am I?" And the whole time, God is saying, "*I* AM."

The only way you can do what you're called to do and fight the battles you're called to fight is not because you are but because God is. The great I AM goes with you.

Switch around the proper nouns—make the statement read "I AM" instead of "Am I?"—and then you have God in the proper position. Then you can take the battle, no matter what you perceive. You can go forward in your calling, no matter how things look. You can move according to His Word, in the direction He is calling you.

Big or small, high or low, you can fight the good fight because God is in His proper place: I AM.

The Israelites' mistake was thinking that they needed God only for the big stuff, when in reality, God is needed in all we do. He makes experiencing the taste of victory possible. Ignore Him, leave His power and assistance unactivated, and your attempts will fail.

Our daughter Kelsey is the sugar monster in our house. She especially loves baking chocolate-chip cookies. The first time she made them, she did it with her mom. Mom taught her. Kelsey put all the ingredients in. Baked them. Took them off the cookie sheet. They looked and tasted good.

Everybody was happy with Kelsey's cookies.

A couple days later, my wife and I walk into the kitchen, where we discovered Kelsey trying to make cookies by herself. Kanika and I looked at each other and said, "*Hmmm*, we don't know how this is going to go." Kelsey wasn't deterred. "This isn't a big deal. I've done it before. Last time, you were with me, Mom. You showed me. So I decided I could do it by myself this time."

It looked like our daughter was putting everything in there, so we let her finish. But about five minutes after she slid those cookies into the oven, the oven was smoking. Literally smoking! After five minutes!

I walked over and said, "Kelsey, what in the world did you do?"

"I don't know, Dad. I used all the ingredients."

Famous last words.

Listen, friends, those cookies looked like crackers. They were cracker cookies. I called them *crackies*.

Kelsey could say, "No, I did it right" all she wanted, but something sure wasn't right.

They were crackies because they didn't rise. They just spread out on the tray, bubbling on top and burning underneath and turning black. It was just a mess. A smoky mess.

We got those crackies out of the oven quick and put them aside, and I said to my daughter, "Kelsey, we missed something."

Her mom went over the ingredients with her. "Honey, you didn't put flour in the cookies. That's why we got crackies. You missed an ingredient, thinking you could do it by yourself."

"Well, I thought I did everything," Kelsey said as she scraped the crackies off the pan and walked toward the trash can.

"Wait, what are you doing?" my wife and I asked. "Where you going with that?"

"'I'm throwing them away," our daughter answered.

My penny-pinching wife and I looked at each other and said, "No, you're not!"

"What do you mean? What are we going to do with them?"

"You're going to eat the crackies," we told her. "You made them. You've got to eat them because we paid for those Ghirardelli chocolate chips, and those two sticks of butter, and that granulated sugar. You decided to go forward without Mom. But we don't waste food around here."

Kanika and I made Kelsey eat the crackies she made so that she could experience the taste, so that the next time she tried to bake cookies, she wouldn't miss the main ingredient.

The main ingredient wasn't the flour. The main ingredient was her mother.

No matter what Kelsey's cooking, if she has her mother, her mother's going to make sure that Kelsey has all the ingredients necessary to cook up the taste of victory when she goes into the kitchen.

A lot of us are having to eat things we've cooked up without God. And we end up tasting defeat when we could be tasting victory.

If only you and I would bring in the main ingredient…if only we'd open the God app and connect with Him, the outcome could be so much greater. He reminds us throughout the Bible, "I have a plan for you, a recipe for victory that I've created. Let Me give it to you instead of you trying to come up with it yourself."

As God's people, we have to stop allowing "Am I?" to determine whether we go forward or whether we quit. Instead, let's start believing, *Whether I am or I'm not, it doesn't matter. The Lord is everything I need to taste the victory in my circumstances.*

The Pain of Pride

Joshua 7:5-7 tells us how bad things got for God's people:

> The men of Ai struck down about thirty-six of [Israel's] men, and pursued them from the gate as far as Shebarim and struck them down on the descent, so the hearts of the people melted and became as water.
>
> Then Joshua tore his clothes and fell to the earth on his face before the ark of the LORD until the evening, both he and the elders of Israel; and they put dust on their heads. Joshua said, "Alas, O Lord GOD, why did You ever bring this people over the Jordan, only to deliver us into the hands of the Amorites, to destroy us? If only we had been willing to dwell beyond the Jordan!" (NASB 1995).

Israel's leaders were experiencing a whole lot of pain. The pain of pride. Joshua is on his face before God, saying, "Lord, it would have been better if we had never come this far. Why did *You* ever bring us over the Jordan?"

Joshua was outright blaming God. He was putting the loss on God when he didn't even bring Him into the picture! Sound familiar? Maybe right now you're echoing Joshua because of the pain you're in: "Alas, O Lord! Why did You…? If only…"

This is what we call *reactive* prayer, not *proactive* prayer. Joshua didn't try to find God during the battle, or at the beginning of the battle. He didn't fall on his knees before God until after the battle was lost. It's how a lot of Christians pray. This is how *I* pray sometimes. I don't look for the Lord until I'm losing. Until I'm going through defeat and difficulty. He hears from me after things have already gone down, not when things are up.

How different would our battles and our lives be if we went to God first in prayer?

Look at Philippians 4:6: "Do not be anxious about anything, but in everything by prayer and pleading with thanksgiving let your requests be made known to God." God is the One who can give me peace. That's proactive—not reactive.

How about 1 Thessalonians 5:17? We're told to "pray without ceasing." That means "do not cease praying." Proactive, not reactive.

Second Chronicles 20:15 says the battle I'm going through is not even mine; it belongs to God. So how can I *not* invite God into it?

First Corinthians 15:58 says, "Be steadfast, immovable, always abounding in the work of the Lord, knowing that your toil is not in vain in the Lord" (NASB 1995). That is proactive.

God is trying to get you to play both sides of the ball. Offense, not just defense.

As Christians, we spend too much time reacting to the culture, to the difficulty, to the battle; reacting to the defeat, the discouragement, the hurt, and the pain. Meanwhile, God is saying, "I AM."

The One who is, and was, and is to come wants His warriors coming to Him constantly, praying without ceasing. Jesus declared in John 15:5, "I am the vine, you are the branches. He who abides in Me, and I in him, bears much fruit; for without Me you can do nothing." He elaborated in verses 7-8, "If you abide in Me and My words abide in you, you will ask what you desire, and it shall be done for you. By this My Father is glorified, that you bear much fruit; so you will be My disciples" (NKJV). That's proactive from start to finish.

Placeholder or Presence?

Why was Joshua on his face? Why was he pleading before the Lord? Because, according to verse 5, "the hearts of the people melted." That means they felt a huge sense of loss and defeat.

I went looking for melted hearts in the Bible. In Psalm 22:14, the writer describes his condition: "My heart is like wax." The reason is given in verse 1: "My God, my God, why have You forsaken me?" Later, in Ezekiel 21, verses 3 and 7 together foretell that the people's hearts would one day melt at learning that the Lord their God was against them due to their wickedness. Just the feeling that God had withdrawn from them would make their hearts melt. The reality of that would be indescribable.

After reading those two examples, I knew the fact that the people's hearts melted in Joshua 7:5 was about more than just a loss in battle. From the loss, they assumed that God had withdrawn from them. And if He was no longer in their presence, then they were no longer in His presence.

I'm sure you've had times where you've asked, "God, where are You?" Maybe you've recently pleaded, "Lord, are You with our country? Where are You with my family? Where are You in my singleness? Are You with our ministry or not?"

When you no longer think the Lord is with you, your heart melts. Your courage fades. Your fears rise. But the Lord Himself has said, "I will never desert you, nor will I ever abandon you" (Hebrews 13:5). Here in Joshua 7 as well, we see that the Lord was there—but Joshua wasn't waiting on the Lord. Rather, the Lord was waiting on Joshua. The Lord had a word, but Joshua wasn't listening.

This happens all the time. We're not hearing God—not because He isn't speaking, but because we're not present before the Lord.

You know how, on Zoom video calls, you have the option to turn your video off? When you do, the screen leaves a placeholder, a façade. You could be off doing something else and still give the impression that you're there. You're not there, of course; it just seems that way.

Not long ago, a couple of my friends used the placeholder on a Zoom call with me, and so I decided to test them to see if they were listening. After explaining my plan, I said, "Hey, you and you, what do you think?"

I could hear crickets out in my backyard, it was so quiet.

Nobody said anything.

Suddenly, the video came back on and they said, "Huh?"— breathing hard because they'd run back in the room to show their faces.

I said again, "What do you think about the plan?" And they said, "Well, what part of the plan?"

Oh! Naha, guys! I only had one part to my plan. It wasn't that elaborate. And so now, even though they were actually there on the video, they both looked like placeholders. They were sitting there staring at me because they didn't know the plan. It's not that I hadn't given the plan. It's that they gave me a placeholder instead of their real selves.

How many of us are doing that to God?

He gets our placeholder on Sunday while we live an alternate life Monday through Saturday.

We put up a placeholder that says, "I'm a Christian," yet all we talk about is the politics of the party we prefer.

We give God a placeholder promising that we're committed to His will, but then we run out into the world and call all the shots without running anything by Him.

Our placeholder communicates all these things; meanwhile, we're going about doing our own thing. And God says, "I've been speaking, but your placeholder is not your presence."

Repositioned

Notice the verbiage in Joshua 7:5 about the thirty-six men who perished in battle: "They were struck down on the descent." This was a tragic loss for the people of Israel. They were struck down on their way down.

Don't you know that being humbled has some pain to it?

When I was playing in the NFL, I was struck down on my way down. I had already been cut, traded, hurt, and carted off the field. Still, I wanted to play. So even though I got a nibble from God, sensing a call to ministry and preaching His Word, I wasn't really listening because I was giving Him a placeholder called the NFL. Even Kanika was saying, "Babe, I think the Lord is calling us away from this. He's given us a lot of signs."

Yeah, you'd think. But my placeholder was up.

Then I got a call from the Kansas City Chiefs, and I said, "See, babe—God's will!"

So despite getting these nibbles, and hearing the same from my wife too, I went to work out for the Chiefs. I took an open door, which tells me that not every open door is God's door. In KC, I started working out with a friend named Cletus. One day, I was running a 40 outdoors, and *boom!* I hit the ground in throbbing pain and grabbed the back of my ankle.

I knew it was bad. Turns out I'd torn my Achilles tendon. And with that injury, my NFL career was over. I felt like God was saying to me, "I'm allowing you to be struck down on your way down because you're not going to continue to walk in a way that I'm not calling you."

Let me tell you, experiencing that pain changed the way I walked. After I had surgery, I put on a boot and my crutches and I limped into Dallas Theological Seminary. God has a way of allowing you to lose so that He can reposition you to win.

Ever since, I've been doing ministry and preaching. This victory—where I'm doing what God has called me to do—came from my loss. It came from me experiencing the pain of my pride.

He says in His Word: Those who humble themselves will be exalted, but those who exalt themselves will be humbled (see Luke 14:11). Falling on your face before the Lord is the right place to go. Every time.

A Reactionary State

Take it from me. It's *always* better to be in His will. Things may seem to be going downhill. Life may have struck, and now you're nosediving fast. Even so, you want to return to the Lord.

I know people who not only stayed in a reactionary state during a difficult time, but who have reacted in ways that are not of the Lord. Some folks react with alcohol. Or drugs. Or by turning to carnal friends and taking a step back from the Christian lifestyle. People react based on their feelings and not the Word. They react in ways that leave God out.

Others struggle with thoughts of suicide: "I'll take care of this myself instead of coming back to the Lord." Yet Jesus already paid the price for their victory. What He wants is for every follower of His to experience the victory He has supplied.

I hope you understand what I'm saying, because too often we run to things that have no power to turn our situation around. A temporary fix does not give you long-term success.

If you've been running to something other than God, let me encourage you to be like Joshua. Joshua was experiencing the defeat and hurt brought on by his own decisions. But he fell on his face before the Lord, the One who has the power to redeem us and our defeats. And as soon as he did, the Lord encouraged him. In Joshua 7:10-13, we read that the Lord told him twice to "Stand up!" (Notice the exclamation point.) He also let Joshua in on something important: there was sin inside Israel. The Lord informed Joshua, "Some of the sons of Israel have taken things from Ai that I said no one should take, and they've kept it a secret." And He reminded His servant: "My people cannot stand before the enemy with sin in their midst" (see verses 11-12).

Because Joshua went to the Lord, he gained awareness of things he did not know—things that could cause further defeat and devastation. Only God can help you see what's happening inside of you that may be causing some of your loss or difficulty.

Now, Joshua didn't know who had sinned or what they'd done (see verse 1). How could he? The battle of Jericho involved many, many Israelites. But had Joshua been proactive, the God who gave him knowledge of things that needed to be plucked out so that he and the people could have victory is the same God who could have given Joshua that information before the battle.

Some people don't just go the wrong way, they don't go to God at all. And so they live without the awareness that would help them understand what to do differently.

From Losing to Winning

Through the power of God and the grace of God, the pain we experience can take us from losing to winning. Thanks to the Lord, our pain can reposition us for greater work in His kingdom.

When the Lord made Joshua aware of sin that needed to be removed, Joshua took care of it. God gave His servant encouragement, awareness, and—as we'll later see in Joshua 8—God would give Joshua a new plan for victory where he had just experienced defeat.

Joshua received all of this because he returned to the Lord, ready to hear what God had to say. We can do the same today, hearing Him through prayer and Bible reading.

No one can see their face without a mirror. The Bible is a mirror that reflects back to us things we may be unaware of. When we stand before the mirror with "unveiled faces," as 2 Corinthians 3:18 puts it, we "[behold] the glory of the Lord." We see God's will more clearly, as well as what we need to know about ourself.

I pray that each one of you will position yourself to go to God in all you do before you do it. Before the problem becomes bigger. Before any unnecessary pain. Before your descent or defeat. And in those times when you forget—and God either humbles you or allows you to be humbled—return to Him as soon as you realize you've left Him out. Not only can He redeem and restore you, but He has a plan for you to defeat what has defeated you.

CHAPTER 6

CLOSE TO THE FIRE

pastor got a call real early in the morning one day. He grog-gily answered, only to be jolted awake by the desperate voice of his assistant pastor, who was losing his mind on the other end of the line. "You need to get up to the church right now, Pastor! Our church is on fire!"

"What do you mean, our church is on fire?"

"Just what I said. Our church! The whole thing is burning!"

The pastor jumped out of bed and drove over. By the time he arrived, the building was a bonfire, its wood exterior burning like tinder. All he could do was stand there and watch with his heart sinking. As he looked around for his colleague, the pastor noticed that a lot of people were standing nearby, watching the church burn. Of course, the police were there, and the fire department—all doing their jobs. But it looked like just about all the neighbors in every direction had come out of their houses and apartments, awakened by the sirens and the blaze. Even people who had been driving down the street stopped their cars and got out to see what was happening.

The church seated only two hundred, but the pastor estimated that two to three times that many folks had gathered. He eyed his associate. "I've never seen so many people at our church before."

The assistant pastor replied, "Yeah, but that's because our church has never been on fire before."

There's something about a fire that draws a crowd. There's something about a blaze that makes people curious enough to stop and see what's going on.

Fire in the Bible represents the presence of God. So wherever there was fire, it definitely got people's attention!

Want a few examples? In Exodus 3, Moses talked to a bush that was on fire—and from it the Lord talked back. If you move on to Exodus 13, the Lord was leading His people through the wilderness by a pillar of fire at night. In 1 Kings 18:38, you have the God-versus-Baal scene where God struck the wet altar with fire to prove that He was the living God who was making things happen.

Even today, spiritual fire signifies God's presence. So the question we should be asking ourselves is, "Am I a Christian who is on fire with His presence? Or am I just making a claim?" The church gets the same question. It's not, "Do we call ourselves a church?" but rather, "Are we a church that is blazing with His presence?"

To fight life's battles, you need holy fire. Every soldier needs a good fire to keep him or her battle-ready.

I'm challenging each of us on this point because we live in a cold, hard world and people are looking for something that makes sense. Some rhyme or reason. In reality, they're wanting the presence of God, but when they go searching, are they finding a fire *anywhere*? What I see happening is that the ones who are supposed to be on fire are just as cold as the ones who are searching. If that isn't true, then tell me: How can we have all these churches with all these members, and all these pastors with all these conferences and workshops, and all these youth pastors and youth conferences, and all these chaplains and ministry teams…and still have all this mess? My dad has made this case many times, and I see it too. We Christians seem to be lacking fire, even though there are lots and lots of us around.

Are you filled with fire? Is your church? That's the burning question.

Abiders Wanted

Until now in this book, I've focused on fighting God's way and some of the important ways He equips us. That was the *equipping* section. Starting with this chapter, we'll look at the *committing*. This is about the internal—how to build up our commitment and our heart toward Him.

The apostle Paul once wrote a letter to some fellow believers, where he talked about drawing down the presence of God individually and collectively as a body. He began one segment of the letter, saying, "For this reason I bend my knees before the Father" (Ephesians 3:14). He was praying on behalf of the church at Ephesus. His prayer was that the Father would grant strength

> with power through His Spirit in the inner self, so that Christ may dwell in your hearts through faith; and that you, being rooted and grounded in love, may be able to comprehend with all the saints what is the width and length and height and depth, and to know the love of Christ which surpasses knowledge, that you may be filled to all the fullness of God (verses 16-19).

Paul wanted himself and all the saints to have power from the inside out. And to know the love of Christ that surpasses the ability to know. He was on his knees praying for a huge delivery, that his brothers and sisters in the church would be filled with the fullness of God. What I observe here, though, is that while Paul was praying for a huge delivery, he started with intimacy. He didn't skip the relationship part.

What's your reason for waiting to really go after God? Did you ever come to Him for delivery but didn't want to bother with the One delivering the package? You didn't want to spend time with the Deliverer?

He desires that we seek *Him* out. In Jeremiah 29:11-13, the Lord says, "For I know the plans that I have for you, plans for prosperity and not for disaster, to give you a future and a hope. Then you will call upon Me and come and pray to Me, and I will listen to you. And you will seek Me and find Me when you search for Me with all your heart." Jesus said in John 15:7, "If you abide in Me, and My words abide in you, you will ask what you desire, and it shall be done for you" (NKJV); and in Mark 11:24, "All things for which you pray and ask, believe that you have received them, and they will be granted to you." The apostle John added in 1 John 5:14, "This is the confidence which we have before [the Son of God], that, if we ask anything according to His will, He hears us."

This isn't any prosperity gospel that I'm talking about. This is the deliverance of the Savior in our lives—what He does in us as we spend intimate time with Him. He is looking for *abiders*. He is looking for people who will get on their knees in front of the Father and press in.

My mom knew a little about abiding. She was from Guyana, South America, where tea parties are a thing. I mean, she wore the white gloves and everything. I'm not kidding! The tea gang does it big!

Since my mom and my grandmother were big tea drinkers, my mom schooled me in the proper ways of tea when I was young: "There are two different types of tea drinkers, Jon. You have me—I am an abider. What I do is, I take my tea bag and just drop it in the water. I don't mess with it. If I leave it alone, the water will infuse the tea and the tea will infuse the water, and they become one. And once that happens, you cannot separate the two. If you just leave the tea bag in there and let it marinate, you will have some strong tea.

"The other type of tea drinker," she said, "is the dipper. These people want to dip the tea bag in and out, in and out, because they think that the darker the water, the stronger the tea. They don't realize that while dipping gives them the color, it doesn't give them the true strength of the tea."

From what I see, there are a lot of Christians who are dippers. They dip in on Sunday and then they dip out on Monday. They dip in for Wednesday night service and then dip out on Thursday, back to the world's ways. But where's the strength in that?

God desires abiders—people who will linger in His presence, remain in His presence throughout each day, knowing that He is worthy. Is He not worthy?

Every now and then, I have to remind myself I'm not just praying. I am going before the Creator of heaven and earth. He is eternally strong and tirelessly steadfast. He is all-graceful. All-merciful. All-powerful.

Is He worthy of our ongoing attention? Is He worthy of an intimate, persistent relationship? No question. God deserves our closest attention. He deserves our deepest intention. Are we dipping or abiding in Him?

We make time for a lot of things. I know most of us are going to make time to watch our favorite TV show—and I'm not talking about me, I'm talking about ya'll! But as I was analyzing my TV-viewing self one evening, I realized, *Wait a minute now. My heart is rooting for immorality to take place.* When I was hit with this, I looked at my wife and said, "What am I doing? My heart is rooting for sin to win!" I had become numb toward immorality. Unmoved and unoffended by constant scandals. Does this happen to you? Do you realize that you're intrigued by ungodliness?

As you spend time with something, it can draw you the wrong way or it can draw you the right way.

If a scripted TV drama can so easily draw us to fictional immorality, how much more can the King of kings draw us to true spiritual intimacy? How much more can He deliver Himself to each of us, strengthening us with power in the inner man? We spend time with some things, but we need to spend time with the right things. Paul says, I can't skip spending time in the Lord's presence; that's where the fire comes from. Jesus and God and the Holy Spirit, as ONE, are fire! That's the Lord's nature. How close to the fire do you live? Is God's power radiating from within you? Do you have the fire, or have you allowed your problems, your pain, or your battles to keep you cold?

Distance from the Sun

In our solar system, Pluto is the farthest planet from the sun. Consequently, Pluto is cold all the time. Matter of fact, scientists are now saying that Pluto is so far away that it really shouldn't be considered a part of our solar system. The sun is on fire, but because of Pluto's distance, it never heats up.

Some Pluto saints are reading this book. Your distance from the Son makes you cold all the time. The people who hang out with you start to feel the freeze because they're in your atmosphere. You're far enough away that if somebody at your job charged you with being a Christian, you might be found "not guilty" based on how you live your life.

Move several planets closer to the sun, and you come to our planet. Planet Earth is seasonal. It is both hot and cold, depending on where it is on its axis and where you live. Sometimes its face is toward the sun; sometimes it turns its back on the sun. You could say it's close enough to the sun to be respectable, but far enough away to not really be bothered with the heat. The heat is manageable.

It's ironic that we live here. Spiritually speaking, many Christians are living a middle distance from the Son, Jesus. The biblical term for being both hot and cold is *lukewarm*. I'm facing the Son as long as things are going well. As long as I'm comfortable and in a good place. I'll be with God as long as I feel that God is with me. Once He starts telling me what to do, though, once I realize He's not going to save me on my timeline, I'm turning my back. I'm going to limit my exposure to the heat.

Then there's the planet Mercury. It's so close to the sun that it's nearly a ball of fire. Am I talking to any Mercury saints right now? You have such a close relationship with Jesus the Son that you're always on fire?

Paul drew near for this reason: he desperately wanted the fire to inhabit God's people. He wanted them to be "rooted and grounded" in God's love. That's how we withstand any battle, any war. To know that kind of enduring, empowering love starts with intimacy. Intimacy lights the fire that never goes out.

A Way of Life

My wife and I were examining the Ephesians 3 text together (she does this with me, letting me bounce ideas off her), and one of the things I noticed in verse 14 was Paul's position when he sought intimacy. He said, "I bend my knees before the Father." Paul acknowledged the greatness of God while accepting his own subordinate position.

How many of us are emphatic about elevating ourselves? How many of us use God to get out of our battles versus serving Him *in* our battles? How many of us only go to God when the battles go our way? We like to rule our own lives and devise our own rules. We have no interest in coming under the Father and His authority. We use Him for comfort and convenience, not for calling.

But there can't be two gods. The Lord said in the Ten Commandments, "Thou shalt have no other gods before Me"—not even you. By insisting on your own way, you push God farther away. And just like with a firepit, the flames ultimately die out if you stop feeding the fire.

Paul was admitting, *I am the subordinate in this relationship*. I relate to his position because of my relationship with my father. I have a healthy fear of my dad for two reasons. Number one, we have a great relationship and I don't want to disappoint him (that's still true!). Number two, I knew growing up that if I messed up, it would hurt. After messing up a few times, I recognized that I needed to go to my dad first. If I did this, then he could sign off on what I was doing. Having him sign off on the front end of my question meant I didn't have to worry about consequences on the back end.

If going to the Father is such a good thing, why then do we ever put Him off? Why make decisions without Him? It seems to me that bowing our knees before the Father should be a way of life. Living close to the Son and responsive to the Holy Spirit should be a way of life. The problem is, for many Christians, our true God is a god called Comfort, and we have made God the servant of Comfort. However, Christian maturity—being able to fight the good fight and keep the faith like Paul did (2 Timothy 4:7)—means stoking the fire, not ignoring it. It means maintaining the fire in relationship even if you have to give up being cradled in comfort.

At Oak Cliff Bible Fellowship, we have adopted sixty-five public schools as part of our community outreach. We provide mentoring and tutoring and family support services to all the at-risk students in those schools, and every now and then, the schools let me come in and speak a word of encouragement to the kids. One of the main points I make about maturity is, "You know you're maturing if you think of yourself as immature." Viewing yourself this way puts you in position to act more maturely because you've essentially said, "I need to learn."

To think that you're mature, that you know all you need to know, keeps you immature—because you won't bend your knee to receive the wisdom and counsel you need. This is why teenagers and their parents often go back and forth on issues. The young people think they know more than Mom and Dad. Mom and Dad are in place to teach them, but kids who won't acknowledge the rule and authority of their parents, who think they know better than their parents, lose out on intimacy within the relationship. Immaturity abounds. Immaturity rules those kids. They fail to understand how life really works. They can't apply truth appropriately because they aren't receptive to truth.

Some of us adults aren't so good at acting our age with God. We act more like teenagers toward Him than adults, refusing to submit and allow God to be God. *I don't need any help. I've got this.* All the while, what we've missed out on most is building our trust and closeness with Him. You need faith in your Leader to withstand the battle. You need faith in your Leader to come out victorious.

So I don't fault the Father at all for letting us sit in our mess every now and then. Sometimes the best thing for us is to struggle until we're worn out with our own solutions, just like a toddler throwing a temper tantrum. Once you're exhausted and depleted, you begin to understand: *I don't need to be making decisions apart from Him. Living away from the fire is no way to live.*

From the Inside

It's important that we hold a subordinate relationship to God, because, let's face it: We *are* subordinate! He alone is God! Coming under His rule grows our intimacy with Him. It draws us nearer the fire and keeps us there.

Paul said he bowed before the Father *for this reason*, that the people of God would "be strengthened with power through His Spirit in the inner self" (Ephesians 3:16). I don't have enough space here for us to examine this verse phrase by phrase the way I'd like to, but one thing I do want to look at is where Paul directed his prayer. He prayed that the believers in Ephesus would be "strengthened with power through [God's] Spirit *in the inner self*" (emphasis added). There has to be a Spirit-to-spirit relationship with God. True power and strength originate from the inside out, not the other way around. You can't expect something to be fulfilled on the inside by coming at it from the outside. However, you can be filled on the inside even if you have battles on the outside.

This isn't some New Year's resolution prayer on Paul's part. You know how we do with New Year's resolutions? We have an idea of what we want to enact starting on January 1, and we figure that by gritting our teeth, we'll make it happen. But then three weeks later, we don't feel like doing it anymore. Those two pounds I lost, I've gained them back and now I'm on to some other way of getting rid of the weight. I tried to do it from the outside in, and I just couldn't sustain it.

Paul prayed that we would be strengthened on the inside, knowing that this is an authentic, steadfast strengthening that will remain consistent through the hardships. Based on 1 Thessalonians 5:23, we have three parts to us: spirit, soul, and body. God is spirit. So in order for His power to be generated inside of us, we have to be plugged in from our spirit to His Spirit—and plugged all the way in.

Maybe this is why things seem broken in our lives. Maybe this is why people think there's no hope: they're not plugged in enough for their faith to activate.

For fighting and winning your battles, the question is not, "Am I plugged in at all?" For the full power-experience, you have to ask yourself, "Am I plugged in *all the way?*"

Do you have a consistent, Spirit-to-spirit relationship with God? Because I promise you, there's power in that socket! If power isn't being generated in my life, it's not the socket that's the problem. It's because I haven't connected to the electrical circuit.

We need to be strengthened with power from the inside to operate with power on the outside. The fire, the electricity, comes from the inside.

During my time with the Buffalo Bills, one of my teammates invited me over to his house. "I want to talk to you," he said. This guy had been in the league for ten years, and I had been in the league for only two, so I thought he was going to mentor me. Pulling up to his mansion, I was excited to be there. He had the whole spread— exactly what you think NFL players have: an eight-thousand-square-foot house, a bowling alley inside; he had the Bentley and a Maserati and other cars. But what he ended up telling me was, "I've been watching you, and I know based on how you carry yourself that you believe in God.

"This is my dream since I was a boy," he continued, motioning around us, "and I was able to accomplish it. And not only did I accomplish it, I've been on the same team for ten years, which you and I both know is rare in the NFL.

"I've got all the money. All the cars. The house. If I don't work another day in my life, I don't have to do anything but go fishing and play golf. I've got all this stuff," he said, "but I have a hole in my heart so big, you can drive a Mack truck through it."

That's when I took him to Ephesians 3 and showed him: If you don't start on the inside, it doesn't matter what you have on the outside. Your outside cannot continually strengthen you.

We are spirit, soul, and body combined. Your spirit gives you the ability to communicate with God, because God is Spirit. Your soul is you communicating with yourself; it's how you know that you are you. The person you are expresses itself through your body. And your body gives you the ability to communicate with the outside world.

That's why Paul was saying, let's start with the Spirit. If we can get our spirit connecting with God's Spirit, then a very different message will be communicated to the soul. And when the Spirit of God starts communicating that message to the soul, the soul will begin to express itself through the body, and you will be able to transform the battle versus being threatened by the battle.

At Capacity

Most of ya'll might know that my dad is a big-time philosopher type. He's an intellectual, a brainy guy who reads at least a book a week. When I was young, he would regularly talk to me about different philosophies and lines of thought. Being the opposite of my father, my attitude was usually, "Who cares?" But I did learn some great lessons growing up.

My dad even went so far as to tell me how popcorn pops! I didn't care how popcorn pops. I just wanted it to do its thing so I could eat. But he would tell me how popcorn works anyway, and every now and then, he'd use it in an illustration like this: "You've got to understand, son, that in each kernel of corn there is moisture. The microwave heats up the moisture that's inside the popcorn. When that moisture is heated up, it becomes steam. Steam rises. When the shell can no longer handle what's going on inside because of all that steam pressing against it—that's when you hear all that popping going on. It's because of what takes place on the inside."

Paul was saying, *I pray you'll be strengthened on the inside* so that you can get heated up by the Spirit. The Spirit will start communicating with your soul, and then, *watch out!* At your church and mine, among those who are Spirit-to-spirit with God, there's going to be some popping going on!

Drawing near to the fire heats you up. Drawing near and staying close transforms you for the battle.

For this reason, we bend our knee.

Subordinate living.

Intimate relationship.

Drawing close.

Abiding there.

Spirit relating to spirit.

It all strengthens our inner man and brings the overcoming power of the Lord into our fight.

A life lived near the fire results in this huge delivery: "So that Christ may dwell in your hearts through faith; and that you, being rooted and grounded in love, may be able to"—watch this— "comprehend with all the saints what is the width and length and height and depth, and to know the love of Christ which surpasses knowledge, that you may be filled to all the fullness of God" (Ephesians 3:17-19).

Through subordinate living and the inner strength that you gain from intimacy with God, your inner self grows in its capacity to take in who God is. All of Paul's talk about height and depth and width and breadth and to know the love of Christ that surpasses knowledge…those are capacity words. God wants each of us and our churches to be the permanent dwelling places of His Spirit. His temples. His full-time homes on earth, not vacation spots that He visits every once in a while.

To be true temples and true warriors, where we are filled with all His fullness, our capacity has to grow. God is able to make that happen, but don't expect Him to expand past your capacity. He doesn't want to waste anything on someone who is wasteful. You have to have the capacity to handle Him, which is one reason we don't experience Him as much as we should. Our capacity is limited.

Have you ever wondered why you might be going through what you're going through? God will often expand your battles to expand your capacity. He wants you to experience more of Him.

Paul was on his knees, praying for greater capacity in the saints, so that we would be able to recognize and live out who God really is.

When Kelsey was little, she asked me one day for some grapes.

"Sure, you can have some," I told her. And I put a few grapes in her hands. Four to be exact.

She looked at the grapes with her little two-year-old eyes, and she looked back at me and asked, "More, Daddy?"

I told her, "You can't handle any more grapes. The size of your hands is only good for what I put in them."

I understood that she wanted more grapes. I understood that she was asking for more grapes. But she wasn't going to experience more grapes because her capacity was just too small. Daddy was not going to waste his grapes. Grapes are expensive, you know? I wasn't about to give her more than she could handle because she wasn't ready. She would have to do something with her capacity in order for me to give her more.

That's what God is saying. Often we come to Him like this. *I want...Can I have?...Give me more.* When we don't see more of Him, the problem is not with Him. Looking at our verses in Ephesians 3, it's obviously not a problem with Him. He is looking at you and me. He is considering our capacity to handle what He has to give, and He's going to give us more only as we grow up and draw closer to Him.

My dad has always said (I'm paraphrasing), "If you bring a thimble to the ocean, you're only going to get a thimble's worth of water. It doesn't matter that the ocean is enormous. Your capacity dictates how much the ocean puts in. If you bring a bucket, you'll get more than a thimble, but you won't get more than a bucket. Try to bring in a barrel or a tanker. You won't get more than either one, because that's what you brought with you. The ocean fills only what you give it to fill."

The amazing thing about the ocean is that the water level doesn't go down when it fills those vessels to capacity. It has so much to give that it's not diminished by the filling. It's just waiting to see what you're going to bring to it.

Paul wanted the saints in the church to not only catch on fire with God's presence but to experience the love of God that surpasses knowledge. First John 4:8 says, "God is love." That means love is His nature, His essence. For Him, expressing love is not dependent on human conditions. He loves because that's who He is.

To even begin to fathom such love means we have to have the capacity to receive it. Paul says it this way in Ephesians 3:20: "Now to Him who is able to do far more abundantly beyond all that we ask or think." Paul is speaking of a great God. He is talking about each of us being filled with the Most High God, the One who is able to exceed our imaginations and not just start a blaze in our hearts and minds but fill us with the bonfire of His love. A bonfire that will sustain us and guide us through every dark night of the battle and every dark valley of the soul.

Once we're on fire, then we can talk about His ability. Because His ability will be seen only through those things.

God is able, says Paul. For all the excitement we feel at the beginning of Ephesians 3:20, watch what Paul describes in the next part. This is one of the church's greatest verses: "To Him who is able to do far more abundantly beyond all that we ask or think, according to the power that works within us."

Whoa now! It's not about what He is able to do; it's about, "Are we ready?" Do we have the capacity to take in what He is able to do? Do we really believe that He can work it out? We sing and shout about how great God is, but we can't experience His greatness until we are ready to absorb His power and integrate it into our problems, fully connected and fully activated.

God longs for us to draw near. He wants us to be a people who draw near individually and as members of His church, so that we can experience Him at a whole new level.

Let me conclude with this little confession. I never wanted to go to seminary. That just wasn't my thing. I've never been a formal learner, and I never liked school. Yet God had been pressing upon my heart, "You need to go study My Word. You need to get in there." I didn't want to, but He and I had been talking, we had been communicating, and against all my objections, I went to seminary.

And you know what? I learned things that I didn't think I had the ability to learn. I realized in seminary that I knew nothing about the Bible. When those professors sit you down and start teaching the Word, and you go deeper and deeper, you're no longer satisfied with the worship service on Sunday. It's no longer *Go to church and then go back to your ordinary life.* You start letting God *be* your life! Because when you experience that fire—I'm telling you, it's a whole different life. A different way entirely, where circumstances are not in control, and God is.

And so my prayer today is that we would bring Him glory by coming to Him and walking in strength. That we would be better than Facebook-status Christians who claim to follow God but who don't know Him intimately. I pray that we would be filled with Him, fired up by Him, and radiating Him from the inside out.

To All Generations

Paul ends this passage with these words: "to Him be the glory in the church and in Christ Jesus to all generations forever and ever" (3:21).

God is concerned about His glory. He wants His people to be a reflection of who He is. When I look in the mirror, I shouldn't see me anymore, I shouldn't just see my pain anymore, I shouldn't see simply the battle anymore. I should see Christ even more because "I have been crucified with Christ; and it is no longer I who live, but Christ lives in me" (Galatians 2:20).

Something interesting happens in NFL locker rooms that very few people know about. Guys on the team will occasionally switch lockers to be nearer to somebody they want to learn from. Which teammates of yours have grabbed up all their gear and made the effort to move their locker closer to yours? Which people in your life, your community, your church or workplace have come to you and said, "I've relocated my locker because I've seen you over here living the life I need to be living. I couldn't figure things out, but moving closer to you has helped me"?

Each of us is supposed to be walking in a very new way. If we're not, then we need to be strengthened in our inner man so that we can begin to know the love of Christ that surpasses knowledge. When people see our fire, through our lives and through the church, the flames will spread and keep spreading "to all generations forever and ever."

So draw close and be filled. This is what will energize and empower you to pass on your fire to the next person who needs it most.

Scan the QR code or visit
https://jonathanblakeevans.com/fyb-film-2/
to view a message from Jonathan.
(chapters 4–6)

CHAPTER 7

MORE THAN A BELIEVER

Many contrary circumstances come with the choice to follow Christ. People call Him by name all the time, especially when they're facing trouble. But to commit to Him as your Lord, who you actually live for and live to serve, that's where it gets real. In God's battle plan, the goal for us is to reach the place in our relationship with Jesus where we're not just believers but disciples—visible, verbal followers of Christ through every storm and difficulty, not just when the waters are calm.

I say that because I owe you the whole truth: once you make the commitment to be more than a believer, expect resistance.

If you read the book of Acts, you'll see that as soon as Jesus' disciples started going out into the world to share the gospel, the world started coming down on them. They were beaten; they were thrown in prison…I mean, things got rough.

I think about my own life and how difficult it was for me to walk away from the NFL. I've told some of my story in *Your Time Is Now* and within this book. The experience taught me a lot. Becoming a disciple means being willing to go against the currents.

Jesus' disciples were about to learn this firsthand. After a full day of ministering to crowds of people, Jesus "compelled the disciples to get into the boat and to go ahead of Him to the other side." Meanwhile, "He went up on the mountain by Himself to pray" (Matthew 14:22-23). Before long, a strong wind rose up on the Sea of Galilee, and these boys in the boat found themselves in a tumultuous situation, a storm.

We get different details as we read Matthew, Mark, and Luke in the Bible. The three books together are referred to as the Synoptic Gospels, meaning they tell the same accounts from different vantage points. In this scene, the Gospel of Mark says the men were "straining at the oars" (6:48), while Matthew's Gospel says their boat was "battered by the waves" and they were facing a "contrary" wind (14:24). In the New American Standard Bible, the textual footnote provides a literal translation for the word "battered" as "tormented." Their boat was *tormented* by the waves. So between both writers, we know that the disciples were straining at the oars, struggling to get any movement, because the winds were fighting them so hard.

Let me tell you something about the trials and tribulations of life. When you're doing everything you can to get yourself out of difficulty but you're getting no movement away from the difficulty, it's probably because God has put you in it. We know that rough times are sometimes the result of disobedience, but not every time. The faithful also face resistance.

In their obedience, the disciples were experiencing contrary winds. Forceful winds that were pushing back at them. While in the will of God, they found themselves straining at the oars in a boat that was being battered by waves. Sometimes it's not until you follow Jesus that you hit the really rough waters.

This is a big reason for making sure that you obey—and build confidence in your obedience. Then you won't be so quick to conclude, "I'm not in God's will," just because things are rocky in your marriage or your job or with your kids.

The rains may be soaking you. Your world may feel unstable. You may be a long distance from land, where you're being tossed around and tormented by circumstances. *And yet you may be in the exact center of God's will.* For the obedient one, the contrary winds and bashing waves can be evidence of your faithfulness.

At another time, Jesus warned His disciples, "'A slave is not greater than his master.' If they persecuted Me, they will persecute you as well" (John 15:20). As with Jesus' own life, you can be obedient…and your obedience may carry you right into resistance. When you follow God, doing what He asks of you, your storm may be a sign of your commitment and calling. A sign that you are His and He is yours.

That's what's here in the Scriptures. If you're encountering contrary winds in your calling from God, you'd best believe He is preparing you for a commission that is contrary to the world's calling. In fact, once you decide to row against the currents of culture and live for Him, that's when you can expect to experience the *most* resistance! All these things coming against you probably mean you're being called to go against these things.

The good news is, God will push you through the very circumstance He's put you in. If He is your "problem," only He can be your solution. If He is the one who brought you here, He's the one who's going to get you out.

Being a Disciple

Jesus was training His men for what was ahead. The disciples needed to have the whole picture because, in a matter of time, they would receive a great call on their life, a great commission. You may know it by heart: "Go, therefore, and make disciples of all the nations, baptizing them in the name of the Father and the Son and the Holy Spirit, teaching them to follow all that I commanded you; and behold, I am with you always, to the end of the age" (Matthew 28:19-20).

These men were about to *go* and *do*. Jesus would soon task them with sharing a message that would offend a lot of people. So for the disciples to find themselves fighting a storm here in Matthew 14 was good practice, because times of resistance call for enormous spiritual persistence. *Great resistance must be met with great persistence.*

Jesus' men were feeling the storm. They were experiencing the difficulty that comes with being a true disciple. And for hours they fought back in their own strength.

Finally, their leader shows up. But not like normal. You'd think Jesus would bring a bigger boat and tell them to climb aboard. *Nunh-uh.* "He came to them, walking on the sea" (verse 25). He came walking on water, like it's the Ice Capades, only no ice. Some of the movies I've seen show Jesus walking on a surface that is smooth as glass. Wrong. Jesus was literally walking on a storm. He was walking on chaos. At the same time that the waves were tormenting the boat, He was strolling on top of them.

What's this about? Well, for one, when we face resistance in our battle, the persistence we need isn't the kind of persistence we see in the disciples. They persisted in their own strength; we need persistence in our faith in Christ. This is another strategy in God's battle plan: *We need to look to Him, not ourselves, for both our endurance and our deliverance.*

I think Jesus chose to walk on water instead of coming to save the disciples some other way because the water was giving the disciples the problem. It was beating up their boat. So He showed up walking on their problem—walking *on top of* the very circumstances that were beating them down.

Your trials may be on top of you, tormenting you, but Jesus wants you to know, "I'm on top of your trials." Your problems may be a problem for you, but Jesus wants you to know, "I am greater than the difficulty you're going through."

The surest way to experience discouragement in our trials is to keep looking to ourselves for rescue. There's just no way we can fight our way out of life's storms on our own. Jesus wants every one of us to know that anytime we get through a tough time, it's not to our credit—it's definitely because of Him. Though we may have been straining all night, we didn't get ourselves out. He got us out. We need complete faith in Him.

Jesus comes to us with all power, walking over the very circumstances that have us bound up in fear. He alone is able to bring us through the storm and take us to the other side, where the skies are clear and the waters are calm.

Why the Wait?

Matthew adds an interesting detail in verse 25. He tells us that it was "in the fourth watch of the night" that Jesus came on the scene. Jesus had sent out His disciples earlier that evening. They got in the boat around 7:00 or 8:00 p.m. The fourth watch of the night is from 3:00 a.m. to 6:00 a.m.

Jesus didn't arrive until at least 3:00 a.m., even though Matthew 14:24 indicates that the disciples were struggling before then. Their boat had been "battered by the waves" for a while. We know this because they were "a long distance from the land."

Once again we're seeing God show up at that breaking moment, just about the time His people are ready to give up. Doesn't this sound like the Israelites at Rephidim when they needed water? The game is almost over, the final whistle is just seconds away, and now here He comes.

Why now? Why wait until the winds were at their worst before making His presence known? Why did Jesus delay until the circumstances were accentuated? Maybe you're in that same boat in *your* life, with the same kinds of questions: "Why has He left me straining at the oars for so long? Why hasn't He helped me before it got this bad?"

It could be because He wants you giving it your best shot. Then, after you have done so, you'll know without a doubt that you can depend on no one but Him.

It could be so that when you give your testimony, what you say will have nothing to do with you and everything to do with Christ. You won't be saying or even insinuating, "I did it." You'll give Him *all* the glory.

And it could be that Jesus will wait till the last moment because He wants you to think He is not only great…but the Greatest; not only true, but the Truest; not only real, but the Realest. Anytime you add the appropriate suffix to His name, you're recognizing Him as being above all—not just above all of nature, including storms and seas, but above all your circumstances, your worries, and your battles.

Saying it another way, Jesus was showing those disciples, and all who would ever be His disciples, *I am God.*

How is it that Jesus was walking on the water? Simple. Jesus is God.

Hebrews 1:2 reminds us that Jesus created the world. Some of you might be wondering: *Then why does Genesis 1 say, "God created the heavens and the earth"?* Well, let me put two and two together for you.

- In John 10:30, Jesus Himself said, "I and the Father are one."

- John the apostle said of Him, "In the beginning was the

Word, and the Word was with God, and the Word was God…And the Word became flesh, and dwelt among us" (John 1:1,14).

- In John 14:8-9, Philip asked Jesus, "Lord, show us the Father." Jesus replied, "Have I been with you for so long a time, and yet you have not come to know Me, Philip? The one who has seen Me has seen the Father." *The one who has seen Me has seen the Father.*

- Then in Colossians 2:9, Paul wrote that "in Him all the fullness of Deity dwells in bodily form."

These are just a few examples, though the entire Bible testifies that Jesus is God.

Jesus was crucified exactly for this reason, for claiming to be God. The religious leaders of His day accused Him of blasphemy. Yet from the start of His ministry, we see Him not only saying that He is God but proving it. Right before this storm that we're reading about in Matthew 14, Jesus had healed the sick and miraculously fed the five thousand by multiplying five loaves of bread and two fish—things that only God can do. Now here He is, walking on top of a tumultuous sea.

Matthew reports that "when the disciples saw Him walking on the sea, they were terrified, and said, 'It is a ghost!' And they cried out in fear" (14:26). They're seeing Jesus, but they don't recognize Him. They're seeing Jesus, but they're terrified. In their perception, this figure coming at them isn't Casper the friendly ghost. It's more like one of those ghosts on Scooby-Doo.

The word *ghost* in this verse means "a distorted reality." Because of what the disciples were going through, they saw the truth as something that it wasn't. Help had arrived, yet they automatically thought, *Oh man, this can't be good. It's another problem we have to deal with, something else that's going to hurt us!* It was Jesus walking toward them—actually Jesus coming to save them—yet they thought it was evil coming against them.

Between the darkness of night, the bad weather, the crashing waves, and being stuck out there in a boat, the disciples' situation looked grim. They feared for their lives. And it affected their vision.

I don't mean just their eyesight but their perception, their mindset. The truth was standing right in front of them, yet the disciples couldn't see beyond their circumstances. Their vision was distorted by what they were going through.

But catch this: "Immediately Jesus spoke to them, saying, 'Take courage, it is I; do not be afraid'" (verse 27).

I love what He does here. Rather than stopping the storm with His words, Jesus stops the storm *inside of them* with His words. He assures them, "It is I—the Truth. Don't worry; you're not looking at some distorted reality. I am coming to save you, not to harm you. Though your circumstances are hard, don't be afraid, because I am God, and I am greater. You see? I stand above all your circumstances."

Jesus' words are a call to faith. A call to trust. A call to understand that the One we're looking at is true, even though what we may be going through is tough.

Perspective Check

It doesn't always take long for a trial to take over and distort our vision, does it? I mean, these boys were out on the water for only a matter of hours.

I took my niece Kariss to the Texas State Fair several years ago, and we went through the crazy house with all the funny mirrors. In front of the first mirror, she said, "Oooo, this makes me look tall." I said, "Yeah, it sure does."

At the next mirror, Kariss says, "This one makes me look short." I said, "It sure does."

In front of the next mirror, she says, "This makes me look skinny." I said, "It sure does."

At the last mirror, my niece says, "Whoa! This mirror makes me look big!" Wanting to joke with her, I said, "Actually, that mirror is real!"

Kariss fell into a trap on that one. Had there been a real mirror beside each of the crazy mirrors, she wouldn't have been sucked in. But after being inside this scenario for a while that was messing with her eyes and her mind, she could be staring directly at the truth and still see a distortion.

That can happen to any of us. Getting a clear view of the truth inside a storm isn't easy. Emotions can fog up our spiritual eyes just as quickly as our circumstances can cloud our vision. The truth is always in front of us, but the grimness of the moment often distorts our response to the One who is able to save us.

Moments like these call for a vision adjustment. Persistence means looking for Jesus in your circumstances, not trying to look through your circumstances for a clear picture of Jesus.

Back when I was playing for the Buffalo Bills, full-service gas stations were still around. You'd pull up to the pump and an attendant would come out and fill up your tank, plus he'd usually wash your windows and check your oil. It was all pretty cool.

Around that time, I heard an illustration about a husband and wife who were driving cross-country. After a while, so many bugs had hit their front windshield that it was just a mess, so the couple pulled into one of these full-service stations. The guy came out, gave them some gas, and then asked, "Is there anything else I can do for you?" The husband said, "Yeah, would you please clean all those bugs off our window?" The attendant grabbed the squeegee and a paper towel, and he cleaned all the windows.

When the attendant was done, he asked, "Is there anything else I can do for you today?"

The driver replied, "Yeah, man, please clean my windshield again. I'm seeing all these specks, and they're getting in my way."

The window looked clean to the attendant, but he was a nice guy. "Alright, let's try again." He did it all—cleaned the front windshield completely, wiped it dry—and asked, "How's that, sir? Is that good for you?"

"No, my window is still gross. Don't you see that? Hit it again with some water!"

The attendant kept his cool. "I don't understand, but okay." He wiped the window once more and squeegeed all the water off. "Is that good, sir?"

The husband was just about ready to lose it. "My windows are still dirty! What are you doing?"

Then his wife reached over, grabbed her husband's glasses, gave them a good cleaning, and put them back on his face. And suddenly everything was clear.

In life, what you're looking through determines what you see. *The lens you use will inevitably determine the perspective you choose.* Especially in times of resistance or pain. As disciples of Christ, we must learn to look at our storms through the lens of truth. Because the truth remains the truth, even when it's tough to see.

I can't tell you how many times I've sat with people who were battling rough times, and as we've talked about what they're facing, they've had this distorted picture of who Jesus is or what God was trying to do through the storm. The storm was so bad that their vision of the truth had been tainted.

Other times, I've pointed people to the truth, and they've treated it as if they just saw a ghost. The truth seemed harmful and scary, so they resisted it. They were looking through the perspective of the pain instead of looking for Jesus in the pain.

Be careful that your trial doesn't make you distort the truth. Rather than viewing your situation through your trial, you have to view it through the truth.

Are you and I going to feel strong emotions during life's trials and tribulations? Of course! My challenge is that we don't lose biblical perspective amid those emotions. It can easily happen if I'm "all in my feelings." I can easily distort the truth or want to run from it.

This is one reason we must be taking in the Word of God every day. His Word clears our vision, helping us to be able to identify Jesus from a distance. His Word also clarifies our emotions. No matter where you are or what you're going through, Jesus will let you know whether you're operating based on your emotions or based on reality. Keep your eyes on Him and His Word.

What Not to Resist

You want to go to the truth, not be afraid of it; you want to run to the truth, not escape it. How many times have you and I distorted God's Word in our fear?

These men saw something true, but they thought they saw something false. People of God, do not distort God's Word just because what you're going through has distorted your emotions. Your reality is distorted because of your circumstance, not because the truth has changed. We have to learn to look past what we see and feel and trust Jesus and His Word. The truth can always be trusted.

I encourage you not to resist the truth either. The men in the boat were so afraid in their circumstances that they were afraid at the sight of Jesus. They were so caught up in their emotions that they were about to start rowing in the other direction. Do not leave your calling just because obedience has put you in a tough situation. You must never walk away from your children, or your marriage, or a chance to forgive, or any situation where God has called you to commitment. Do not deny God's Word just because your emotions are stirred up. Do not reject Jesus just because you can't quite see Him right now. He may seem distant, but He sees you. Through conditions like these, He is inviting you to practice His presence so that you can recognize and respond to Him in any setting.

Once you place your life in His hands, you're no longer going to justify disobedience. You're no longer going to choose an ungodly course of action because of your circumstances. You'll look past your circumstances and your emotions for the truth. You'll be looking to Jesus and looking for Jesus in the middle of your storm *and* in the middle of your future mission from Him.

Bringing the Peace

During those times you've faced resistance, you've probably wished for something practical, something real, that speaks to what you're going through. Well, this is as real and as practical as it gets. In your trials, you need two things—the truth of Jesus' presence and the courage of Jesus' presence. When you have those, you will have godly persistence and peace.

God's battle plan has this huge benefit: You can have peace during life's storms. "Take courage, it is I; do not be afraid," He told His disciples (Matthew 14:27). Do you see how Jesus went to the inside right there? He spoke peace to their inner man—to their emotions, intellect, and belief, all at the same time—yet without changing their outward circumstances.

Sometimes I've cried out, "God, please forget all that inner stuff. I want You to change what's going on around me. I need You to make everything go smoother. If You'll just fix my circumstances,

I will be better on the inside." But Jesus proved we don't need ideal situations to be unafraid. He promised His presence along with a "peace...which surpasses all understanding" (Philippians 4:7 esv).

Why is it a peace that surpasses all understanding? *Because I don't understand why I have peace!* It doesn't make sense from the world's point of view. Things can be chaotic on the outside, and yet I can be at peace on the inside.

Have you ever experienced a peace that surpasses understanding? The storm is still raging around you. The wind and the water are still a problem. Everything's a mess. But somehow, you're okay. You have this peace on the inside because you've allowed the Word of God and the presence of God to calm you. The storm is howling and the trial is on you, but none of it consumes you. That is the peace of God at work, guarding your heart and mind in Christ Jesus (4:7).

I guarantee that when you're exhibiting a calm like this in a hurricane, others will notice. People will look at you and ask, "How can you be going through this much storm and have this much peace?"

How can you? Because it's Him, the actual Truth, not a ghost.

How can you? Because Jesus is real, and you know His Word is true.

How can you? Because He is God, and you know He is greater than your circumstances.

You're no longer cowering at some distorted reality. You have courage because of your confidence in Christ, not because the seas are calm or you're a strong rower. You are okay because of who He is. That's ultimately what Jesus was saying to His disciples.

This reminds me of one of my favorite movies, *Inception*. I don't know if you've seen it, but it's one of those films that gets you thinking. Leonardo DiCaprio's character could enter dreams and operate within them, but then he could also enter the dream's dream, and then enter the dream within the dream's dream—which got really confusing to me after a while because I didn't know where he was.

Is he in a dream? Is he in reality? What helped is that he carried a totem, like a toy top, with him. It was an objective standard that let him know which world he was in. He'd spin the top, and if it kept spinning, that meant he was still in the dream world because tops slow down and fall over after a while. If the top fell, that meant he was back in reality.

He didn't measure his reality based on his perception. He measured his reality based on an objective standard.

We have to put our trust in something objective because, subjectively, we mess ourselves up whenever we see through our trials instead of seeing our trials through Jesus.

He is every Christian's standard for measuring reality. You feel like you're defeated? Measure that reality by Jesus Christ. "We overwhelmingly conquer through Him who loved us" (Romans 8:37). You feel like you've been abandoned? Measure that reality by Jesus Christ, who promised never to desert or abandon you (Hebrews 13:5). You feel like the storm is drowning you? Measure that reality by Jesus Christ, who's walking on top of the storm straight toward you.

He and He alone can deliver peace, whether or not He delivers you from the circumstances that are upon you. He alone can use your trials, your hard times, the resistance you face to show you a clear view of who He really is. So take courage and do not be afraid.

In the middle of your storm, see Jesus and know...He is with you, He is speaking peace to you, and He will see you through.

CHAPTER 8

FROM SAFE TO FAITH

Sometimes Jesus will let the storm rage from dark till dawn in order for someone to recognize who He is and take a step toward Him. We see this going on with one of the disciples in the boat as we return to Matthew 14. This guy decided he was done with the uncertainty. He was ready to make a move toward faith, saying, "Lord, if it is You, command me to come to You on the water" (verse 28).

That's my boy Peter. For him to say, "*If* it is You," means he still wasn't sure he could trust his eyes because the darkness was so dark, and the rain was pouring, and the waves were hitting so hard..."but let me go ahead and test this out." That was his attitude. "I'll take my chances on the truth. If it's actually You, Jesus, then I'll know I've put my trust where it belongs."

That's the thing about storms. The truth can be tough enough to see that even disciples can be unsure. Yes, you believe in Jesus. You know His story backward and forward, and you've read through the Bible a couple of times. Jesus has even identified Himself in your struggle and said to you, "Take courage, it is I; do not be afraid" (verse 27). But when it comes to stepping out and testing out this whole faith thing, you're thinking maybe you'd rather stick with the other disciples.

In Peter's mind, trying out the truth was better than being stuck in contrary winds. *Why not try something different and go somewhere than stay in the boat, straining with my homeboys, going nowhere?*

I'm challenging you to be like Peter rather than his friends. He chose to be an eagle, wanting to be what God had created and called him to be. And Peter chose the right thing.

We don't really hear about the other guys until the end of the story. Those dudes were more concerned about the weather around them than the truth in front of them. They cared about staying safe in their boat.

Some of ya'll have been hanging out with that crowd too long. You look like them. Walk like them. Talk like them...even though you've been given wings to soar. Every time you're at church hearing the truth, something inside you makes you nod your head. Something inside you whispers, *Yeah, what the Bible is saying—that's the direction I should go.*

That's the eagle, wanting to use his wings. That's the right thing.

Will you take the risk, even if the truth is a little hard to see in your storm? Whether you soar or not depends on how willing you are to step out of that boat and test the wings God gave you.

The Truth Test

For those who care to know what's real, the call of truth is strong. Strong enough to make a strong-willed guy like Peter give up his seat, leave the boat, and set out in its direction.

How do you find out if the truth is the truth? Simple. Put it to the test. Ask the truth to help you do something you could never do without it.

In this circumstance, Peter asked of Jesus, "Command me to

come to You on the water" (verse 28). In your own life, go to God in prayer and ask Him to help you accomplish something you've never been able to accomplish on your own. Go to His Word, learn what it says about your problem, then apply His wisdom. See if God allows you to start walking on top of circumstances that, without Him, you've nearly drowned in before.

You're dealing with sexual addiction? Substance abuse? Marital issues? Stop trying to fix it yourself. Test the truth.

You've done everything you can think of to reconcile with that person you're estranged from? You can't seem to commit to anyone in your dating life? See what God's Word recommends, and then give *that* a trial run in real life.

Having trouble controlling your anger? You've tried biting your tongue and gritting your teeth but you just can't conquer this thing? You're the loose cannon who can't figure out how to calm yourself down despite the anger-management classes? See what the truth says and walk in it.

I dare you. Take a chance on Jesus. Really study His Word and trust what it tells you. Put all your weight behind what He says. Rely on your divine Helper, the Holy Spirit, like you never have—and see if the truth doesn't transform your life. Because in Matthew 14, Jesus is showing His disciples, *What's hard for you is nothing for Me.*

Stepping Out

A long time ago, my dad installed motion-detector lighting at the church. The reason is, people who don't have to pay the bills don't worry about turning off the lights! So to save on electricity, Dad had one of those companies come in and set things up.

You know how these lights work. You walk in the room and the power detects movement. *Bing!*—the power comes on. Once the movement in the room stops, the power goes off.

The power is contingent upon the movement. There's always power in the air, but if there's no movement in the room, everything stays dark. You read me? You have the opportunity to activate the power at any time; it's just that nothing's happening where you're sitting. The power will be activated as soon as you move, because that's what the power does. It responds to movement.

Peter wasn't one for staying in the dark. He wasn't one for putting just a toe in the water to activate the power either. He was an all-or-nothing, type A kind of guy who liked jumping in with both feet. So he said, "If it is You, Lord, command me to come to You on the water."

Jesus responded with one word that encompasses the Christian life for every one of us: "Come!"

He didn't give a dissertation explaining who He is. He didn't preach a thirty-minute sermon. He didn't need to. He had one word for His disciple: *Come!*

Whether you're a slow starter or someone who dives in headfirst, your experience hinges on that word. Whether you choose to step out or to stay behind depends on that word. *Come* determines whether you activate the power or not. It determines whether you experience all that God can do in your stormy circumstances—or whether you don't.

When Peter heard that word, he took the chance and stepped in the water. He moved toward Jesus. Lots of people hear the word of the Lord at church every Sunday, and on their favorite preacher's podcasts during the week, but they're not about to take any risks. Until you take a chance on the Word, though, you can't discover if what you're hearing is true enough to stand on. Until you take a chance on the Word, you won't witness what it can do in your life.

Give Jesus a chance. Leave the boat and step in.

Taking that first step toward Jesus not only brings you closer to

Him, but it increases your faith for the next step and the next one after that.

Jesus used *come* in other settings too. He told the crowds in Matthew 11:28, "Come to Me, all who are weary and burdened, and I will give you rest." Yet another time, He warned that those who "are unwilling to come to Me" will not receive life (John 5:40). So if you come to Him, you get rest. If you don't, no rest and no life. Whether you receive or not has everything to do with whether you rely on the authority and power that reside in Jesus Christ.

I remember going to Dallas Mavericks games with my dad when I was younger. As the team's chaplain, he gets preferred parking at the stadium, close to a private entrance with access to a private elevator. He eats in the private lounge with the players and is permitted in their locker room. As long as you're with him, you get to piggyback on the authority that comes with him being the chaplain.

But if I come to a Mavericks game with my buddies instead, I'm going to pay for parking, pay for a ticket, stand in long lines for all the security and ticket checks at the public entrance, and then take a bunch of twists and turns in the stadium to get to my seat—and I'll probably be watching the game from the rafters.

I'll have other complications too. I'll have to pay for food, and it will be what they serve at concessions, not the gourmet selections they have in the players' lounge. Between ticket checks and stepping around the other people in our row, my buddies and I will experience blockages. Why? Because we didn't come with my dad. But if I come with him, I get to access the power that resides with him. This doesn't happen because of who I am. It happens because of who he is.

The moment you come to Jesus is the moment you can begin to experience the power and authority that are His. It doesn't happen because of who you are. Peter knew there was no way he could walk on top of the waves that were beating up the boat. He could do that only if Jesus was who He said He was. "If You are the truth, Jesus, if it is You with me and not a ghost, not some distortion of the truth, then I can do what I could never do before by Your power."

Friend, if you want salvation, Jesus says, "Come!" If you want forgiveness, "Come!" If you want to overcome your trials, heal your marriage, learn how to forgive, come to Jesus. If you don't want to be worried all the time, "Come!" If you're tired of living in fear, "Come!" But you have to decide, *I'm going to leave the boat of my circumstances and trust Jesus.*

Peter couldn't see Jesus clearly due to the storm, but he heard clearly: *Come!* That's all he needed. As soon as he heard the word, Peter was up and out of the boat.

That's faith. Faith functions even when you can't see. It looks to God as if God is telling the truth. Which He is!

I like how my father describes it: "Faith is acting like it is so, even when it's not so, so that it might be so, simply because God said so." Whether you can see the truth fully or whether it's fuzzy—that's irrelevant. God said it, so do it. Trust Him! At the moment you listen, actually listen, and respond in faith, the fog will start to lift. The truth will begin to come alive in your situation. You'll experience personally that the truth has more power than the trial. And that makes all the difference for those who will act on it.

One time not so long ago, there was a fire in a small apartment building. The first responders thought they got everybody out, but then they learned that a little girl named Lisa was still inside, somewhere on the third floor. She was feeling around in the heavy smoke, trying to get to a window, but disoriented and confused. Finally, Lisa found her way. It took all her strength, but she was able to crack open a window enough to escape from the front side of the building.

The problem was, she was still three stories in the air, and the ladder truck couldn't reach her.

As she lingered on the edge of the windowsill, Lisa heard the firemen shouting for her to jump. "We'll catch you!" they yelled. "Our inflatable pad will catch you!" But she was blind and couldn't see where she was jumping.

She was getting more and more scared as the voices grew urgent. She could feel the heat at her back, and smoke was choking her lungs, but fear kept her in place. Then, out of the crowd, she heard another voice, one she knew as sure as the sound of her own. "Lisa, jump!"

It was her father's voice, coming from directly below her on the ground. He was standing at the edge of the pad, and he was calling to her, helping to guide her. "You can do it, honey. Just jump! We're right here!"

Little Lisa took a big breath and did as her daddy said, and a few moments later she was wrapped in his arms, safe at last.

One of the firemen asked her later, after the fire was out, "What finally got you to jump?"

"My daddy's voice," she answered.

His voice had given her the courage she needed because she knew she could trust her father.

I can't imagine what that was like for Lisa, to leap from a burning building onto a target she couldn't see.

I can't imagine what the step onto crashing waves in the middle of a storm was like for Peter either. But knowing that it was Jesus calling to him gave Peter the courage. He probably took a big breath too—and in an instant he was walking on water! Toward Jesus!

It didn't last long though. According to Matthew 14:30, as soon as he reached where Jesus was, Peter started paying attention to the storm again. He noticed how boisterous the winds were. They were howling and creating a racket, just like Satan tries to do. And you know what? Peter felt afraid all over again, and right away "he began to sink."

Every time I read that, I want to say, "C'mon, Pete, you were walking on top of water! You were just now playing free, thanks to the One who made you free. Why would you ever return to the fear, man? Why would you go back to focusing on your circumstances?"

I saw this over and over during my time in the NFL. Some of the guys lived for game day and couldn't get enough of it, and some of them couldn't enjoy anything about game day because they were worried about what the video might show the next day. This big weight was on their back, and they could never let it go.

Those were the players who reached the end of their career...and missed most of it. They let the experience slip right on by because they were looking at the coaches. Looking at the crowd. Looking at the film. Looking at the guys competing for their position. They were worried about yesterday and tomorrow—crucified between those two thieves.

To anybody who's stuck there, Jesus says, "Look at Me! If your eyes are on Me, I'll get you walking on top of this thing that right now has you scared."

Peter took his eyes off Jesus, and as soon as he did, the water started to pull him under. At that moment "he cried out, saying, 'Lord, save me!'" Matthew tells us, Jesus pulled him right back up "immediately." With no delay. Jesus "reached out His hand and took hold of him" (verses 30-31).

Some of us wait until we're already underwater before we even think about Christ. Not Peter. The second he began to sink, he begged for help and got his eyes back where they belonged. Do it at the beginning. Ask for His help. Don't wait until you're gasping for air.

He Is Greater

Matthew 14 says that "immediately" Jesus grabbed Peter with His hand. I'd say that for most of us, it takes something like this, right? We don't fully recognize the Truth until He pulls us out of a situation where we're drowning.

As Jesus was helping Peter back up, He rebuked him, "You of little faith, why did you doubt?" (verse 31). That's what Jesus said as He was taking Peter to the boat. "You have little faith."

Now, why would He say that to His own disciple? I mean, Pete was just walking on water! That takes real faith, doesn't it?

Exactly the point! Peter had just been *walking! on! water!* Strolling where no human has ever strolled. Why would he suddenly look back at his surroundings?

If Jesus had felt like elaborating, He could've easily said, "I was showing you that I am greater than all your circumstances. All you had to do was keep stepping toward Me."

Let me put it in perspective so we don't get too self-righteous regarding Peter. He was believing, and at the same time, *he could not believe what was happening!* That's what caused him to revert to fear.

Every one of us has done this in some version. A relationship can be going well, but as soon as the hurts of the past come into play, what do some of us do? We start acting like we can't believe it's real, and we sabotage it.

We may be walking strong in our marriage, but as soon as we start thinking about the storms of the past, they can creep into our current success.

Basically, Peter caused another storm for himself when Jesus had already put him on top of the real one.

Thankfully, Jesus was there, and He rescued His disciple from the chaos. As soon as He and Peter came aboard the boat, the storm stopped. And everybody gathered around and worshiped Him, saying, "You are truly God's Son!" (verses 32-33).

That day, all those guys learned who Jesus is. Peter most of all.

Before every Cowboys game, Coach Garrett always told the players, "Show them who we are!" He wanted his men to go out there and give the other team fits so that their opponent would recognize who was greater.

Jesus gave His own men fits. He let His disciples go through the scare of the storm to make sure they saw who they could trust.

His guys finally got it. And once they got it? Storm over. Because in seeing Jesus for who He was, they also learned something about how to walk on their trials.

Peter is the one who took a chance that day. All because he heard a word: "Come!"

Jesus had told all the men in the boat, "Take courage, it is I; do not be afraid." Peter is the only one who took Him up on it. And he did it before the storm had subsided. We see in Peter's response most of all that as a believer, you can step out with authority and walk on top of your circumstances once you recognize that the Truth is with you.

Friend, the Truth is with you. Don't miss this moment. With everything you're experiencing in the storm, God is preparing you not just for a great commission but for a great promise. That promise can sometimes get dark, but Jesus is inviting you to set aside your fears and come to Him. Take the risk and decide, *I'm going to leave the boat and trust You, God. I'm going to activate this faith and access Your power.*

You hear His voice, right? That means it's time for your rescue. It also means it's time for you to experience where He's taking you. Step out with your eyes on Jesus. Step out and don't ever stop walking with Him.

CHAPTER 9

BUILDING FOR
THE FORECAST

One of my brother Anthony's colleagues in the music industry grew up in the Midwest and then moved to the South as an adult. She's seen a lot of very bad weather in her lifetime. Especially tornadoes. Some of the storms she's been through have made her extra-vigilant when severe weather is in the forecast.

She's got the local weather app with 24/7 radar. She checks the sky from her office at work, where employee safety is one of her job responsibilities. She and her husband keep a couple flashlights on hand for when the power goes out. And inevitably, if her friends or family are in the storm's path, she will forewarn them. In fact, her family calls her "Doppler 6" because she's like their very own in-house meteorologist.

That's a family that is prepared for storms. When the wife and husband built a house a few years ago, they made sure they had an interior space, away from windows, where they could take cover when the winds kick up. They have ordered their lives and built their house knowing that severe storms *will* come. But they've also done all of this with the intent of withstanding the weather.

Jesus directed us to do this spiritually. "In the world you *will* have tribulation," He said (John 16:33 ESV, emphasis mine). Some Bible versions say "trouble," but "tribulation" captures it better. Other translations get even more specific: "you will have suffering…persecution…sorrow…distress." Those are words that indicate war in the atmosphere above you. A clash of cold and warm fronts. It starts above you, but before you know it, it's coming at you.

The spiritual war started with a clash between Satan and God in the heavens, and then it came to earth, first with Satan's fall, and then with Adam and Eve giving in to the serpent, causing the fall of creation. As the Son of God who walked this earth with us and defeated sin, suffering, and death for us, Jesus knows what is coming *at* us better than anyone. He's been through it. He's the expert at surviving brutal conditions. That's why we ought to listen and take heed when He sounds the alarm.

Before His own suffering and persecution on the way to the cross, Jesus alerted His disciples about what kind of weather to expect and how to prepare for it. With a parable, He set up a simple contrast they could relate to, explaining what life looks like for those who take His storm warnings seriously and for those who don't.

In His preaching and teaching, Jesus often used parables—earthly stories with a heavenly meaning—as illustrations. I want to take us through a parable the way Jesus painted it so we can understand and apply it to our lives.

The Sermon and the Servant

Some of you church cats who grew up in Sunday school will know this one, from the Gospel of Luke, chapter 6 (also in Matthew 4–5). It's the Sermon on the Plain. He preached this right after choosing His twelve disciples. They were all there that day, along with a "great multitude" of people who had gathered around Him to hear Him and to be healed of sickness and unclean spirits (verses 17-18).

Verse 20 says that Jesus "raised His eyes toward His disciples" and then spoke the familiar words of the Beatitudes: "Blessed are you who are poor…who are hungry…who weep…Blessed are you when people hate you…on account of the Son of Man" (see verses 20-23).

That should've been their first hint about what they'd signed up for. Storm clouds were on the horizon. *You'll be poor, hungry, sad, hated because of your relationship with Me*, He said. *Ultimately you'll rejoice, but a lot of bad weather is coming first.* As Jesus taught about the nature of His kingdom, He spoke of how different it is and how different we must be in our conduct as disciples of His. Then He concluded with a parable. A parable of two men who built houses on different foundations.

Now get this. His first statement to introduce the parable was a scorcher: "Now why do you call Me, 'Lord, Lord,' and do not do what I say?" (verse 46).

That's how He starts it, y'all! It sounds to me like Jesus packed a little attitude with it too. I can't blame Him. He was the weather reporter looking at the radar a couple of states away, and He knew: *What's coming for you as My followers is no joke. People get hurt when they disregard the storm forecast. I'm telling you that a tornado's aimed right at you. So why aren't you taking cover? A hurricane is closing in, but you're doing life as usual. Why?*

He was trying to wake them up, and if it meant shaking them up with a shocking forecast, so be it.

Now, we know He had great compassion for the lost and the hurting. Many people were healed that day. But Jesus also saw right through the users. He knew who was and wasn't genuine. Judging by His opening shot—"Why do you call Me, 'Lord, Lord,' and do not do what I say?"—there must have been a lot of insincere listeners in the crowd.

In the language of Jesus' day, *Lord* meant "Master," which logically suggests there's a servant somewhere in the picture. You can't have a master without a servant. Yet many of the people who were calling Him "Master" weren't abiding by His words. Jesus' reasoning was, *Why bother giving Me this title if you won't obey Me? That's what calling Me "Lord" means—you serve Me. Yet you don't do anything I say!*

I'm afraid He would find similar fault in the church today. We have people calling themselves Christians who are supposedly submitted to Christ, but you sure wouldn't know it by their actions. They want to build a life according to their codes and specifications, a life that serves themselves, and still they'll pray that God blesses it. Predictably, when storms come and they're not finding a spouse or closing the deal or getting the financial stability they wanted, they'll blame Him—and then keep living by their standards. "Because, you know, God needs to adjust to my lifestyle."

I sometimes have this problem with my kids. If you have kids, you understand. They call me "Dad," which indicates I'm the boss. I have authority. "Dad" means I put a roof over their head, food on the table; I supply their needs. But as soon as I tell them to do something they don't like, the title they call me by becomes irrelevant. Through their actions, they signal that they're willing to disregard me if I don't let them build their little kingdoms the way they want to.

You know you've taken yourself out of position anytime you start expecting Jesus to adjust to your schedule and preferences. You're no longer thinking of yourself as His servant but as a god.

Jesus was warning that you can't have it your way and His way. Either He is your all in all or He isn't. If Jesus is your all in all, then He is Lord and Captain, Master and King. He is Lord of your life, Captain of your ship, the Master you serve, and the King over your kingdom. You work for Him and you build by His rules. His method seems harsh until you learn His motive: "If anyone loves Me," explained Jesus, "he will follow My word; and My Father will love him, and We will come to him and make Our dwelling with him" (John 14:23).

Remember, Jesus knows what's coming our way, and He's forewarned us because He loves us. He knows what's necessary to survive the strongest winds, and He's given us the master plan, a plan that fits the Father's specifications for protecting us. Jesus has walked the way of the Servant Himself. He lived what He preached, coming to earth and carrying out His Father's instructions from start to finish. His true followers reveal themselves in the same way: by not only following His lead but following His commands.

Do you want to know the life God blesses? Do you want to have a life that makes you unshakable? Do you want a house that won't fail at the first storm that comes along? Listen to your Lord. Commit to your King. The servant's life is built on solid ground.

What Makes Sense

Jesus' question in Luke 6:46, "Why do you call Me, 'Lord, Lord,' and do not do what I say?" is something we should be asking ourselves more often. It doesn't even make sense to do one but not the other. The two things don't go together. Ultimately we have to pick a side.

Imagine that you're with the Dallas Cowboys. You go out on the field wearing the silver-and-blue, but you run the Philadelphia Eagles' plays during the game. Who would ever do that, right? "J, that's stupid! No way would I go out there in a Dallas uniform and run the opposing team's playbook." Okay, then, how in the world can you wear the uniform of heaven but run the enemy's plays?

Or imagine that you take the field with that proud star on your helmet, but you make up your own plays, as if the Cowboys had no playbook at all. Again, you'd scoff at this—"That's crazy talk, man! I would never waste the opportunity to play for America's Team!"— except I can tell you for a fact that people do it every day spiritually speaking. They're given this incredible opportunity to play for the Kingdom's Team, but they're following a playbook they wrote themselves. (By the way, don't ever trust a playbook whose author is named Me, Myself, or I.)

By the work of Jesus Christ, you are on the team. You've been chosen and drafted. Wear the uniform proudly and run the plays right. Between His Spirit and the entire Bible, He's made sure you're equipped with everything you need to win. Neither one will ever mislead you. But you do have to let *Jesus* lead you.

Of course, most of us don't like the idea of being told what to do. We want to be our own person—make our own decisions, our own calls. But really, whoever you work for is your master. A servant works for somebody or something. By that definition, we're all in the same situation. It's just a matter of, who is your master?

If you spend your life working for money, then money is your master. If you spend your time pursuing fame and notoriety, then fame and notoriety are your master. If you're going after the fancy title or that nice car—if that's what drives your decisions—then you have a master.

Realistically, you and I are going to be servants to something. But I would rather serve a God who will never leave me, a God who is eternal, a God who speaks words of warning and prescribes the way to blessing—than to serve all the things in life that are temporal, that can be set on fire, that make me popular with people one minute and unfriended, unfollowed, or trolled the next.

Those things are in opposition to how Jesus told us to live. They were never supposed to be our master. Jesus didn't mince words about this:

- "No one can serve two masters…You cannot serve God and wealth" (Matthew 6:24).
- "I am the way, and the truth, and the life; no one comes to the Father except through Me" (John 14:6).

In other words, "I am your Master, I am your Way, I am your Boss, I am your Resource, I am your Lord. And nothing else should have My spot!"

The Eternal Foundation

Right after His bruising statement in Luke 6:46, Jesus shares His parable about building for storms, and His advice is: Build your house strong. If you build it strong, it will last a long, long time.

> Everyone who comes to Me and hears My words and acts on them, I will show you whom he is like: he is like a man building a house, who dug deep and laid a foundation on the rock; and when there was a flood, the river burst against that house and yet it could not shake it, because it had been well built (verses 47-48).

There *will* be torrential rains, He says. There *will* be flash floods. (Notice His words: "when there was a flood"; He wasn't saying "if.") Who will survive the hit when the weather forecast comes true? The one who built on rock.

Jesus offers three elements for an eternal foundation: Everyone who *comes*, *hears*, and *acts* is like the man who built on the rock. No coach asks his players to just come and listen. He asks them to get on the field and run the plays, and if they can't do that, there's going to be a problem. If a coach expects his players to show up and do what they've heard, then why would Jesus Christ's expectations be any less in His kingdom? Don't just go to church and be satisfied with listening. Get to work! Dig deep and do as He tells you! He is the Master Builder after all. He knows what it takes to construct a house that will still be standing after the storm has passed.

The Head Coach in heaven isn't invested in players who just like to sit on the bench. If they don't care about executing on the field, His attitude will be, *Yeah, that's not someone I can use for My kingdom. They aren't interested in winning, and they really don't care about the game plan.*

The fundamental question is, will you execute? Once you come to Jesus, and you hear His words, will you do them?

This is the difference between a Christian and a disciple. A Christian believes in Jesus. A disciple believes *and* follows Jesus with his or her actions and decisions. You can look at a true disciple's life and know that this person believes in Jesus without them saying a word. "Christians," on the other hand, often have to tell you or you wouldn't ever know.

That's what gets me: We wouldn't put up with that anywhere other than the Christian life—"Oh, you know, I believe in Jesus and all that church stuff, but I've got to do my thing too." Christianity is just about the only religion where a person is allowed to believe something, live the opposite of that, and people are okay with it. Everywhere else? That's a no go.

Let's say that you believe you can bench 315 pounds eleven times (that's what I could do when I was in the NFL). Yet if you don't ever work out, your belief doesn't count for anything. Your belief will be nullified by the fact that you don't ever train against resistance. Eventually people will get on you for it: "How are you always talking all this noise about what you can do, but you're not able to do it when the weight is in your palms and it's time to push?"

Players, get that out of here! How are you going to believe something and not walk in it? Have the same attitude toward your commitment to God that you have with everything else in life. Come. Hear. Then do what you say. Live what you believe so that you can be prepared for every kind of opposition you will face.

Jesus' expectation is that when He puts you on the field against a defense called "the Storms," a defense that's daring you to move forward, you'll know what to do with the ball. "You believe you can make the play, so go do it! Stop talking about how good the defense is and get on with running My play calls. I've heard you for a while now. It's time for you to show up with your game. Put your money where your mouth is."

Digging Deep

The one who comes and hears and acts, Jesus says, is like the man who digs deep and finds a rock—a solid foundation—and builds his house on that.

Remember, He is forewarning about the rain and waves and winds because He can see what's coming. Dismissing the forecast over a drizzle of rain is one thing, but Jesus is talking damaging weather. Pounding rain and waves. Flash floods. How can you hope to survive the storms if you're not ordering your life based on what He says? How can you expect to withstand all the weather that's in the atmosphere around you if your house isn't built to last?

To do what God says to do means you're digging. You're not doing what comes naturally, just making something up or taking the easy route. To live biblically, you literally have to deny yourself.

For example, if you want to get out of trouble, the natural response would be to lie. But a disciple of Christ will put in the work to honor God and tell the truth. As a result, his house cannot be brought down or even shaken when the rains come and the torrent bursts against it.

In comparison, the one who only comes and hears Jesus but doesn't do anything about His words, that person is like the man who builds his house without a foundation in a flood zone. And great will be his fall. As soon as the rains come and the river rises, his house will be carried away by the currents.

> But the one who has heard and has not acted accordingly is like a man who built a house on the ground without a foundation; and the river burst against it and it immediately collapsed, and the ruin of that house was great (verse 49).

This is one reason more than 50 percent of our marriages end in divorce; and people everywhere are in debt; and some would rather be jobless than work for a wage…because they're building but not digging. They want what's easy. They'd rather live by their own codes and specifications than God's. And so they pick a plot of grass, set up some drywall with a roof, and they move in. But they'll have no place to live after the first big thunderstorm. A couple inches of rain and they'll be homeless.

Jesus says in Luke 6:48-49 that the person who digs deep will find Him, the Rock. So when the storms come—temptations to sin, life's struggles, things not going your way—you're not easily shaken. You understand that all things work together for good for those who love Christ and are called according to His purposes (Romans 8:28). Because you decided to dig deep, you're standing strong in the middle of a storm.

Somedays, you may feel as if construction is going way too slow. But you know what to say to yourself in those times, because Jesus has spoken to you as you've built. You know that He will be faithful to complete the good work He has started in you (Philippians 1:6). You understand that if you meditate on God's Word day and night, and keep living by it, you will be like a tree that is firmly planted by streams of water, that yields its fruit in season, and its leaves do not wither (Psalm 1:3).

Everybody is chasing peace. I want to have peace, just like you want peace. But peace doesn't mean the sun is always shining. Peace means that you're always shining even when it's raining. Peace doesn't mean that everything's okay. Peace means that when everything's not okay, you're okay.

The man who didn't dig deep and build on the right foundation? You know who he is because when everything falls apart, he falls apart right along with his circumstances.

The One Left Standing

We read the same parable in Matthew 7.

> Everyone who hears these words of Mine, and acts on them, will be like a wise man who built his house on the rock...And everyone who hears these words of Mine, and does not act on them, will be like a foolish man who built his house on the sand (verses 24, 26).

Both men hear Jesus' warning; both of them build a house; both of them go through the same storm: "The rain fell and the floods came, and the winds blew and slammed against that house" (verse 25). The nature of the storm in this case must have been a hurricane, because those guys clearly built right next to the water. But only the wise man's house withstood the storm: "yet it did not fall, for it had been founded on the rock" (verse 25). The fool's house "fell—and its collapse was great" (verse 27).

This indicates something I need to know. A wise man can come to church and a fool can come to church. A wise man can build a life and a fool can build a life. Wise men go through trials and tribulations, and fools go through trials and tribulations. So, at least on the outside, everybody looks the same. We're all going through the same types of struggles, doing the same sorts of things. In fact, put all of us Christians in a room, and you'll see: everybody is there, everybody is listening.

At what point does it become evident who's who—who is the wise man and who is the fool? At what point will the foundation each of them is resting on be revealed?

In the storm.

The storm will out you—every single time. Whether you fall apart or remain standing will be seen.

It's coming.

The one who hears the Word and acts on it is founded on the rock. This man, this woman, is not easily shaken.

The one who hears and does not act, that builder just wanted to do his life his way. No time for digging down to rock and setting a foundation. He's too busy getting that money, enjoying the fast life, making a name for himself. But one day, things will go downhill, and he will blow right out of there, and mighty will be his fall.

So let me ask what Jesus was asking: Which builder are you? You don't have to say anything. We'll just wait till the storm comes and find out.

Though I don't want to go too far into it, what Jesus is talking about in both of these parables is the end judgment. The storm is Him coming back. When Jesus returns, He will judge every person, and when He judges, He will base His decision on the choices we've made.

Some people are going to have a well-built house with a solid foundation, and the judgment won't shake them because they were founded in the right place. Those who just wanted to build according to their specs will have to face the same judgment, and nothing they stood on will still be standing.

That's the eternal side of it, when Jesus returns. Then there's the practical side, our response to Jesus today. Both are in view in this text.

Storms will come. They come for all of us. You're going to face them—without a doubt. The question is, when they come, what kind of foundation will you be resting on? Which builder are you?

Scan the QR code or visit
https://jonathanblakeevans.com/fyb-film-3/
to view a message from Jonathan.
(chapters 7–9)

CHAPTER 10

STEP BACK

By now I hope you're seeing that whether we're facing enemies or the stormy circumstances of life, faith in God and His Word gives us the battle advantage. Nothing can replace an active faith. Instead of running out of juice the more we use it, like our smartphones do, faith increases! The more we draw on it, the more God supplies. And the more He supplies, the more it powers up and energizes us for the missions He sends us on.

Something that working on this book has driven home for me personally is how eager God is to add courage to our faith. He's always ready to give us the boldness we need to follow Him into battle. But how ready are we to even try that "by faith, not by sight" thing (2 Corinthians 5:7), that "do not lean on your own understanding" thing (Proverbs 3:5)? This is what the Christian life (and the spiritual fight) comes down to: In God we can trust. It's us that we have to trust less.

Are you going to trust what your eyes tell you or what the Lord tells you? Are you going to rely on your perception or the Holy Spirit's direction? Are you going to insist that God's solutions and strategies make sense to you? That they look like what you're used to? Will you step forward only if His methods track with what you've traditionally done? With what has worked in the past?

Don't you dare lock Him in like that, as if He has to fit inside some suitcase you're lugging around! The biggest victories happen when we open up our lives and get out of His way, giving Him free rein to not only lead the fight but to win it however He wants to.

This is one of the things Joshua will show us as we return to his story. Walking by faith never fails. You may look like a loser, but looks can be deceiving when God's people operate within His battle plan.

Running for Victory?

In case you think I'm making things up, I'm referring to Joshua 8:15, in Israel's second battle at Ai. It says, "Joshua and all Israel pretended to be defeated before them, and fled by way of the wilderness." Simple verse, simple concept, but it has huge implications for our faith in times of battle.

First, let's understand that this is where Joshua begins to enact *God's* plan. Right before this, as we already saw, Joshua came up with his own plan—thinking Ai could be conquered apart from the Lord—and Israel was smacked down and sent home. Here in Joshua 8, God lays out a plan for victory, and it calls for Israel to conduct an ambush (verses 1-8).

To carry this out involved situating a large ambush team (about five thousand men) west of Ai, while the main army of twenty-five thousand or so set up camp to the north. Joshua and those warriors would purposely camp in clear view of the city, to make Ai's king think they were staging a frontal attack.

This battle plan was the opposite of Joshua's previous plan, where he'd taken only a few thousand men with him, believing Ai would be an easy win. This battle plan of the Lord's was also the opposite of Joshua's instincts as a warrior. God's plan called for the army of Israel to run. To pretend they weren't going to fight. The difference is, this time they would operate completely by faith. God had arranged a victory for His people, but it meant that Joshua and his men would need to retreat. Take a step back.

Moving in Reverse

God's strategy here illustrates the challenge that faces everybody who follows Him. The crux of being a Christian is the battle between our old self and our new self. We are constantly deciding, *Am I going to step back and operate as the new me that the Bible talks about—"I have been crucified with Christ; and it is no longer I who live, but Christ lives in me" (Galatians 2:20)? Or will I keep pushing ahead and doing things the way I always have?*

When Paul wrote his letter to the Galatians, he was facing problems that made him feel like he used to, but he was no longer responding like he used to. Anytime you're facing problems that make you feel like your old self, you need to remember: You're crucified with Christ now. God has given you a new way to win your battle. He's calling you to step back in faith and give Him lots of room to maneuver.

The Lord wasn't interested in Joshua stepping up and being a warrior at Ai the second time around. He wanted Israel retreating, pretending to lose, so that His divine power as the one true God could be displayed. Had Joshua kept messing with God's plan, had he kept moving forward when the Lord said, "Fall back," then Israel would have lost to Ai again. It's Deuteronomy 20:4, "The LORD your God is the One who is going with you, to fight for you," and 2 Chronicles 20:15—"The battle is not yours but God's"—combined in one scene. God had prepared a clear path to victory. *Joshua, move out of the way!*

What happened with Joshua will happen to you whenever you make yourself vulnerable to God's word. It could be the word of His biblical commands, His will, or the direction of the Holy Spirit, but as you execute what God has told you to do, the enemy will see you. The enemy will assume you're finished. The enemy will start to close in like it's game over. Verses 14-16 of Joshua 8 confirm that Ai's king did exactly this; he saw Joshua and his army and pursued them.

That's perfect from God's perspective. For you to take a step back in obedience creates a vacancy, a place within the battle for Him to occupy so the situation and the enemy can be ambushed. However, what He has waiting to replace your plan won't take its step forward unless you willingly step back.

Not everybody bothers to back up. Not everybody will pretend to lose. That's why many Christians are living in actual defeat right now—they've refused to reverse their steps. That was me with my NFL plan. Retreat was my last resort.

The Lord's direction in Joshua 8 was probably the last thing the seasoned warrior hoped to hear. Yet this wasn't Joshua's battle. God wanted His servant to be obedient, not instinctive. God wanted His servant operating on faith, not on what he felt was best. Israel had lost the last time Joshua tried that. The warrior wasn't taking any chances this time. *I'll do the God thing instead of the fighter thing. We will follow the plan and be runners, even though we'll be laughed at. Even though it's not how I've been trained. Even though it makes me feel like a fake.*

And you know what? With this new plan, God positioned Joshua to experience victory—to taste redemption—where he had formerly known defeat.

Emptied

Anytime you step back from doing what you want to do in order to do what God wants you to do, you're advancing. You may feel like you're pretending, it may look like you're losing, but you're actually moving toward the goal line. His way works because God can be trusted. His plan is the right plan for victory. Isaiah 55:8 reminds us, "My thoughts are not your thoughts, nor are your ways My ways." His strategy may not make sense to you, but it's right because it's His.

Jesus Christ is the perfect example of stepping back so that the Father's plan could step forward. He "emptied Himself" is how Scripture says it. He emptied Himself and became a servant, "being born in the likeness of men" (Philippians 2:7). It had to be hard enough leaving heaven and becoming human. Now add in the way Jesus was treated, and if I were in His shoes, I sure wouldn't want to be stepping back. Jesus was almost pushed off a cliff in His own town by His own people. Others tried to stone Him. The people that He came to save—the people that He in fact created—eventually killed Him. Wouldn't you want to retaliate?

Yet in Luke 22, He prayed the ultimate prayer of reversal: "Not My will, but Yours be done" (verse 42). It's not that Jesus didn't desire a different route to victory. In fact, He admitted, "Father God, if there is any other way, let this cup pass from Me. I would like to take a step forward if You'll provide another plan." But the will of our heavenly Father is every Christian's compass. So Jesus forfeited His desire, entrusting Himself to God's plan. *Not My will, Father, but Yours.*

You know what happened. The Son of God was publicly put to shame and crucified. His enemies saw how vulnerable He was, and they came at Him harder. While Jesus was being betrayed and mocked and beaten, it looked like He had lost. While He was taking His last breaths on the cross and being pierced with a spear, it looked like the kingdom of heaven didn't have a chance. But wouldn't you know it? "God raised Him," says Acts 2:24! On the third day, God raised Him from the grave, giving Him all authority in heaven and on earth. Soon after, Jesus was seated with His Father in the throne room of heaven.

The perceived loser won big. In Him, all the fullness of God dwells (Colossians 2:9-10). The so-called underdog is "preeminent" in all things, as the theologians would say, meaning that Christ surpasses all others. He is number one in every way. He owns first place now and forever (Colossians 1:18). There is no greater Champion, for through Him, everything in heaven and on earth is being eternally reconciled, recovered, and restored (1:15-20).

Taking a step back and doing God's will—prioritizing God's plan over any other plan—gave Jesus even greater victory. Not only did He conquer death but He delivered the ultimate win to everyone who would ever look to Him in faith. Hebrews 12:2 calls Him "the author and finisher of our faith, who for the joy that was set before Him endured the cross, despising the shame, and has sat down at the right hand of the throne of God" (NKJV).

Let me say that backwards.

- Jesus sits at the right hand of the throne of God.
- Why? Because He despised the shame; He didn't care how He was perceived.
- Despising the shame, He endured the cross and was crucified—the ultimate act of dying to self.
- Why? For the joy set before Him, the joy of faithfully completing His mission and doing His Father's will.

Jesus trusted that God the Father had a good plan in place, a winning plan. Winning always means there will be celebrating afterward. And so Jesus could say from the garden of Gethsemane, "Regardless of the score right now, Dad, Your will is Mine. It feels like I'm losing, and everybody in this city will think Your kingdom is finished. Still, I'll step back because You told Me to."

The Upside-Down Kingdom

What did stepping back mean for Joshua? It meant having to be a runner rather than a fighter. God would give Joshua victory, but He was waiting on Joshua to stop acting like he had in previous battles. God may be waiting on you as well to take a step back from your plan or your past, leaving room for Him to step in and surprise the enemy.

Have you done that? Have you gotten out of God's way yet? Or are you still standing in His spot?

Sometimes we keep getting beat back down because we've stepped into God's territory, where we don't belong. I can't say it any more simply than, we are not God and we can't win our battles alone. Not with our brains or our brawn. He's telling us like He told Joshua, "Stop fighting and get out of My way."

It's not as unusual a strategy as you might think. Jesus said in Matthew 16:25 that anyone who tries to step forward and save their own life will lose it, but "whoever loses his life for My sake will find it." Matthew 23:12 says that those who exalt themselves, wanting to push themselves higher, will be humbled. Meanwhile, those who humble themselves will be exalted. Philippians 2 backs this up, explaining that because Jesus emptied Himself to the point of death on a cross, "God highly exalted Him." Because Jesus emptied Himself, facing persecution, rejection, and humiliation, God "bestowed on Him the name which is above every name" (verses 7-9).

The kingdom of heaven is the upside-down kingdom, where apparent losers and pretenders come out ahead by the time the battle is over.

How Hard Could It Be?

According to Joshua 8, the king of Ai played right into God's plan; he saw the Israelites in a vulnerable state, just outside the city's front gates, and prepared his men to attack. The home team came out to do battle the next morning, and Joshua's army, pretending to be beaten, soon retreated. Their retreat drew Ai's fighting men—all of them—outside the gates. Not one man stayed behind to guard the city. This left the entire place wide open for Israel's ambush team to invade and burn Ai to the ground (see verses 10-29 for the entire story).

Don't miss this. Had the Israelites gone forward first, instead of going backward, they would have been defeated again. That step backward positioned them for the win.

There's something else here biblically that I'm not going to ignore. Joshua 8:15 says, "Joshua and all Israel pretended to be defeated." How could he ever pretend to lose? Simple. He knew he was going to win. You can't pretend to lose and actually lose—that's not pretending! Pretending to lose means knowing you're going to win.

God had guaranteed His servant the victory in Joshua 8:1-2, "See, I have handed over to you the king of Ai, his people, his city, and his land...Set an ambush for the city behind it." Retreating from the fight wasn't any real risk for Joshua. He knew that's how God would conquer their foes. *So how hard could it be for Joshua to have faith?* That's what you're thinking, right? *God gave our man Josh the strategy: ambush the enemy. It's easy to do anything if you know you'll come out the winner. But I'm different than Joshua.*

Are you? Are you really?

Romans 8:29-31 declares that "those God foreknew he also predestined to be conformed to the image of his Son....And those he predestined, he also called; those he called, he also justified; those he justified, he also glorified. What, then, shall we say in response to these things? If God is for us, who can be against us?" (NIV). Paul stated in Philippians 1:6, "I am confident of this very thing, that He who began a good work among you will complete it by the day of Christ Jesus."

With assurances like that, it seems to me that God has given *you* victory too, not just Joshua. It seems to me that God has already promised, "You're going to win." So there's no reason for you to fear having faith, and there's no reason for you to think that you have to be the warrior in every circumstance. Today, just like in Joshua's day, the battle is the Lord's, and God has guaranteed victory for those who execute His battle plan.

Really, that's the Christian life, isn't it? We have to learn the wisdom of obeying the Lord's words in Jeremiah 33:3: "Call to Me, and I will answer you, and I will tell you great and mighty things, which you do not know."

Of all the trillions of things we do not know, one thing is guaranteed, 100 percent: *God works in mysterious ways; yet His ways always work.* So if God is in it, if He has ordained it, then what looks like losing right now is actually you winning.

Listen to me, kingdom men…listen to me, kingdom women. You've already won! The reason we keep pushing forward to defeat Ai is because we don't believe it; we don't believe we've won. The reason we keep forcing ourselves ahead—trying to handle things using our own intellect, our own ideas, our own people, our own money—is that we don't believe the victory is already ours.

The reason you keep striving to get yourself out of your situation there on the front side is that you don't have faith that God has already set up something on the west side. But I can look you in the eye and tell you: He will give victory from the west side if you'll step back from the front side.

It's really an issue of believing that what God says is true. Because if you believe that His words are true, and you believe that you are already a victor, then you may have problems, but your problems won't have you. That was essentially what Jesus expressed in Luke 22:42 in the garden of Gethsemane: *This is really hard, Father God. I feel it. Nevertheless, not My will but Yours be done.*

You know why He could do that? Because He knew He'd won!

Why go out and try to defeat something you've already beat? How are you going to go get the victory when you've already got it? It can't get much more frustrating than to search for something you already have.

I can't tell you how frustrated I was looking around the house the other day for my phone. I'm running around, checking everywhere. Finally I asked Kanika, "Babe, can you call my phone?" She did, and it rang. In my back pocket. Trying to go get something you've already got is an exercise in futility.

Warriors, what are we doing? We're supposed to be fighting *from* victory, not for victory!

Why are you so stressed? You can be stressed or you can rest—the situation is still the same. If you operate on feelings, you'll be stressed. If you operate on faith, it doesn't mean that you won't feel any pain, but at least you can actually rest in the Lord. He says in 1 John 5:4, "This is the victory that has overcome the world: our faith." He says in Psalm 55:22, "Cast your burden upon the LORD and He will sustain you," and in Zephaniah 3:17, "The LORD your God in your midst, the Mighty One, will save…He will quiet you with His love" (NKJV).

These verses say to me that God is standing ready to take responsibility, but He will not take responsibility from those who won't step back. Because as long as you don't step back, your situation is still occupied *by you*! And as long as it's occupied, God's ambush can't come in.

Step Back 183

You've already won! The game is over. Stop sitting in defeat. At God's leading, you can move in reverse and pretend to lose because you know that these maneuvers create a vacancy for the Mighty One to secure the victory.

Looks Don't Matter

Another thing we must catch here is that Joshua was not concerned with the perception of victory. Rather, he was concerned with the reception of victory. In other words, looks don't matter.

In this era of social media, too many of us Christians are more interested in seeming to be victorious than in actually being victorious. *I don't want counseling. I don't want accountability. I don't want to go to rehab. I don't want to do any of that because then people will see that I'm hurting. They'll find out that things aren't working out.*

You have to retreat from your pride and quit worrying about how you're viewed. Because once you're no longer caught up in the perception, you'll step back from yourself, and God can then actually give you the win.

There are way more people worried about the perception than the reception. They're worried about the wrong thing, and that's why they aren't winning. They're worried about the wrong thing, and that's why they can't rest.

When you make yourself vulnerable to God's word, when you submit to His battle plan, you're going to be seen, and people will make all kinds of assumptions. But at least you will win.

During my travels prior to the pandemic, I always assumed that anybody who boarded a plane with a mask was sick. *Something must be wrong with them.* But once people started masking up during the pandemic, that's when I realized that most of them weren't wearing a mask because they were sick. They were trying to protect themselves from passengers who might be sick. In other words, they were the healthy ones!

In this situation, these travelers were not concerned with the perception of health. Their concern was for the reception of health. They were willing to appear to be sick in an effort to stay healthy and protect themselves.

Joshua pretended to be defeated. He wasn't worried about the perception that he'd lost the battle; he was focused on the victory. And the victory is exactly what he got.

My friend Jeremy Hurd is the greatest high school quarterback of all time. At least that's my opinion. He was the quarterback for Duncanville High School, and I remember him like it was yesterday because I looked up to him so much. He attends my dad's church in Dallas now, and he never really knew this back then, but he was my guy. I would be blocking for Jeremy, and then I would see his number 13 go whizzing by, and while I was blocking my opponent I'd also be watching Jeremy because I was a fan. He could run like a 4.3 forty. Every game was another highlight reel: *Look at Jeremy. That boy is fast! Tear 'em up, 13!*

In those days, we ran the option offense. For those who don't know football like that, let me explain. It's real easy. It means that the quarterback has an option on the play to keep the ball or to pitch it to the running back. His choice. One time, I missed my block terribly on the option play, and my guy hit Jeremy so hard, the whole crowd groaned. It looked like Jeremy had lost big. And when I tell you it looked like Jeremy had lost big, I'm saying BIG! His face mask was twisted to the side; his shoulder pads were unbuckled. I mean, my QB looked like he'd been in a horrible accident.

Everybody was holding their heads and saying, "Ooh!" And then suddenly the crowd said, "Whoa!" and everybody cheered. I was confused. I didn't know what was happening. I'm looking at

Jeremy, who's looking like a loser, and everybody is cheering. Then I looked up and saw our running back headed down the sideline. Touchdown!

Jeremy had taken the option before he took the hit. He took the option and pitched the ball. So even though he looked like a loser, the Duncanville Panthers were winners.

I'm letting you know today that you have an option. You have the option to keep the ball and take the hit, or to pitch the ball to the One who can actually score. God is waiting. It's your choice, your option, but let me remind you, it's His battle.

As you're struggling right now to figure out, *Should I pitch the ball or should I keep it? Because I really need this to end. I'm really suffering*...let me help you: Pitch. The. Ball. For heaven's sake and for your sake, get out of God's way! Step back from who you are and what you want so you can create a vacancy for the Lord to step forward as who He is and do what He does: win big.

CHAPTER 11

RAISE YOUR JAVELIN

Every one of us wants to end with victory. That's where we want to be. But sometimes, as every master strategist knows, waiting within the battle is half the battle. Winning has as much to do with timing as it does with execution.

Joshua had stepped back at God's command. He and his men had fled into the wilderness after provoking the men of Ai. Now it was time to see what God would do. We pick up the scene in Joshua 8:18-19 (ESV).

> Then the LORD said to Joshua, "Stretch out the javelin that is in your hand toward Ai, for I will give it into your hand." And Joshua stretched out the javelin that was in his hand toward the city. And the men in the ambush rose quickly out of their place, and…they ran and entered the city and captured it. And they hurried to set the city on fire.

I get excited about all of this because it's go time in so many ways. By God's grace, we're watching Joshua conquer what formerly conquered him. Israel's leader allowed his previous loss to catapult him into his current victory. That's what we all want to do. We want to let our losses be learning experiences that further our faith in God so that we can win where we've previously known defeat.

I'm proud of Joshua. I'm proud of him for not letting his past mistakes control his current circumstance. We all need to grow to the next level. If I have one prayer for us, it's that even if we face the same battles, we won't be the same in the battles we face. I pray for us to learn, grow, and go on to greater trust in the Lord like Joshua did. He was defeated last time, but he was about to be the victor this time.

Drawn Away

The word "Then" that begins verse 18 points us back to verses 15 and 16. With the men of Israel pretending to be beaten on the north side of Ai and then fleeing by way of the wilderness, "all the people who were in the city were called together to pursue them, and as they pursued Joshua they were drawn away from the city." Verse 17 says, "Not a man was left in Ai or Bethel who did not go out after Israel. They left the city open and pursued Israel." They ran after Joshua, leaving their home completely unprotected.

I want to make sure you understand what happened. The men of Ai were drawn away. Joshua ran away, in obedience to God. But the men of Ai were *drawn* away.

Being drawn away is different than taking a step back. You take a step back because God is asking you to. Being drawn away means you lose your covering. Being drawn away means you're exposed. Being drawn away means you've left your security behind.

The fortunate thing that I see in this text is that Joshua is once again doing things God's way. He took a step back—and the opposition began to be drawn away. Joshua's obedience was like kryptonite to his situation.

No doubt Joshua's obedience to God made Joshua feel vulnerable. Sometimes (maybe most of the time?) being obedient can make us feel exposed. But don't you know that God can use your vulnerability to make your enemy more vulnerable than you are? God was baiting the enemy. "I want you to run away, Joshua, but it's for a purpose. When the enemy is drawn away, they'll lose their protection."

Here's another advantage to doing what God says. As soon as your opponent is drawn away, you're in the very best place to win. Once the battle moves outside the city walls, beyond the enemy's fortification, your enemy is in trouble. By God's plan, and through your obedience, the enemy becomes susceptible to defeat under the weight of its own aggression. You and I are under the covering of God. Thanks to Him, there is victory inside of our vulnerable obedience.

The Bait

Listen to me: Joshua's obedience baited the enemy. It's what the Lord used to reel the enemy in. Joshua and the people of God were the ones casting the line, and the men of Ai were the ones taking the bait. The sad reality today, though, is that it's usually the other way around: Christians are taking the bait and our culture is casting the line. Or our circumstances are casting the line. Or Satan and his forces are casting the line.

Some of us are letting ourselves be drawn away. We're being baited out of our protection. We're letting our hard times lure us out from under God's covering. But we cannot afford this! Because as soon as the men of Ai were drawn away, they were wide open to defeat.

Rather than taking the bait, God calls His people to try taking the risk. The risk of faith.

If you look at Exodus 14, Moses took the risk when the Israelites were caught between the Red Sea and Pharaoh's army. He was in a situation he couldn't get himself out of, but he followed the Lord's command and held the staff of God high in the air. And wouldn't you know it, God split the Red Sea and made it possible for Israel to walk on dry ground!

They walked in the way of the Lord. And when they walked in the way of the Lord, it baited the enemy. Pharaoh's army rode in after the people of Israel and got crushed by the waves. In obedience Moses cast the line, and Pharaoh's soldiers fell for it hook, line, and sinker.

God's people cast lines; we don't take bait.

I know some of you want to leave your situation right now. You've said you're done. You feel like you can't do this anymore. But I implore you, take the risk of faith. Don't take the bait.

I know some of you are angry in this moment. You feel bitter and unforgiving and you want revenge. Take the risk of faith. Don't be the one who takes the bait.

I know that for some of you, your money is running low, and you're at that scary point where you'll do just about anything to make ends meet. But take the risk of faith, not the bait. Don't leave God's cover to try to gain your victory.

We cast lines. We don't take bait.

Joshua cast the line. All of Ai took the bait.

Keep allowing your circumstances to take the bait, okay? Not you. Make sure you're taking the risk of faith. It's a whole lot better to be covered taking the risk than to be uncovered taking the bait.

As we've discussed a little already, sometimes you're going to feel weak against your enemy. But as long as you're following the Lord's lead, understand that God is, in truth, weakening your enemy. God is weakening your circumstance when you feel weak against your circumstance. He is using your faithfulness to lure your enemy away from what protects it.

It was the people of Ai that were drawn away. God's people weren't.

Have you made yourself susceptible to defeat? Are you allowing your circumstance, or someone who is against you, to draw you out? God is telling us all through this account, "Be obedient, people of God. Don't be drawn away."

You don't have to be. In Deuteronomy 5:33, Moses admonished the people of Israel (I'm paraphrasing here), "If you walk in the Lord's ways you will live. Your days will be prolonged. It will be well with you if you obey Him." Deuteronomy 11:25 says that your enemies will not be able to stand against you if you obey the Lord. Translation: Just obey God. Though you feel vulnerable, your vulnerability to Him and His Word actually makes your enemy vulnerable and assures your victory.

It's Time

Back to Joshua 8:18: "Then the LORD said to Joshua, 'Stretch out the javelin that is in your hand'" (ESV). *Stretch out your javelin toward your situation.* Why? "Because I am going to give victory into your hand."

It was time. God was ready to rid Joshua of this circumstance.

Raising the javelin would signal to the ambush squad that it was time to attack. It was, in effect, a victory flag. A rallying cry. "Time to move in." Joshua raised his javelin to let them know the wait was over. What God had arranged was about to be activated. It was time for His people to invade this circumstance, invade this city, set it on fire, and see the victory.

Now, this javelin wasn't the track-and-field kind you see in the Olympics. It wasn't that straight, thin, metal toothpick-of-a-spear that we're used to. Joshua held up a scimitar, which was a long, curved blade coming out the end of a wooden handle.

Let's remember the key locations in this battle. Joshua was on the north side of Ai. The ambush team was on the west side of Ai, far enough away that they couldn't be seen by the sentinels of the city. How would the men on the west side know that Joshua had raised his javelin on the north side? Well, this was a time that a scimitar came in handy—the person holding it would reflect the sun with that long, curved blade. The plan was that the men waiting in ambush would see the gleam of the sun off the sword, and they would know, "It's time to go light the city on fire."

What am I telling you to do? I'm telling you to raise your sword, your scimitar. To lift up God's Word by living out His word in the middle of your circumstance. Based on Ephesians 6:17, the sun— the Son, Jesus Christ—reflects off the sword of your life. And when the Son starts reflecting off your sword in heavenly places, He signs off on your prayers from His seat at the right hand of the Father. He signs off on your obedience because it reflects Him. And in the Father's perfect timing, whatever that may be, He pushes the Go button on your victory—His game plan.

As the army of God, it's time for us to raise our swords in the way we live. It's time for you and me to raise our javelins. First, this signals to God that we've heeded His commands. "I'm committed to Your word, God. I'm living underneath Your covenant. And I've stepped back, just like You said." Second, raising our javelins lets our fellow soldiers know that victory is at hand.

The Theology of *Suddenly*

I want you to notice what verse 19 says in the NASB: "Then the men in ambush rose quickly from their place, and when [Joshua] had reached out his hand, they ran and entered the city and captured it, and they quickly set the city on fire." Twice in the same verse—"quickly."

Don't you know that God can move in your circumstances *just that fast?* I call it "the theology of *suddenly.*" Have you ever noticed this taking place in the Scriptures?

Acts 2:2 shows the Spirit of God moving in an instant. It says, "Suddenly a noise like a violent rushing wind came from heaven, and it filled the whole house where they were sitting."

The Lord says in Isaiah 48:3,

> I declared the former things long ago,
> and they went out of My mouth, and I proclaimed them.
> Suddenly I acted, and they came to pass.

In 2 Chronicles 29:36, the Israelites were restoring the temple after it had been sitting for ruins in years. "Then Hezekiah and all the people rejoiced over what God had prepared for the people, because the thing came about suddenly."

God can move suddenly in your singleness. He can move suddenly in your marriage. He can move suddenly in your finances. He can move suddenly in your purpose, so that you can advance His kingdom.

God can move in your circumstances like lightning. But maybe He is waiting on you to raise the javelin. Before He will advance past GO and send in the soldiers, maybe He is waiting on you to reflect His Son. Then He'll set your circumstances on fire.

Where There's Smoke...

Joshua 8:20-21 offers these details:

> When the men of Ai turned back and looked, behold,
> the smoke of the city ascended to the sky, and they had
> no place to flee this way or that...When Joshua and all

Israel saw that the men in ambush had captured the city and that the smoke of the city ascended, they turned back and killed the men of Ai.

The smoke of the city ascended. That was a signal back to Joshua that he could stop running and return to being a warrior. It's like God was saying, "I know I told you to take a step back, but now you can take a step forward and finish the battle."

Now it's time for you to go back and apologize. Make the call to mend the relationship.

Now it's time for you to go back and heal the marriage.

Now it's time for you to go back and see your calling through.

When you raise your javelin and send the signal to God, God will send the signal right back to you: "It's on. It's happening. Your circumstances are about to change. The enemy is going down."

One time a friend of mine who I'll leave unnamed called me about a situation he was struggling with.

"What's up?" I asked.

He said, "JE, man, I'm hurting."

"What's going on?"

"My supervisor is treating me so bad at my job, I can barely stand it. He's lying to me and he's lying to the staff, trying to silence me and marginalize me in their eyes. It's gotten so bad, I feel like I'm not useful. He doesn't want my opinion in meetings, even though I'm trying to help. Whatever he's said, it's made some people quit speaking to me, when all I'm doing is giving the truth.

"Now the higher ups are putting restrictions on *me!*" he continued. "The governing board has given me a list of rules to follow, and I have to see a counselor. It's a bunch of different requirements. I want to quit, JE. That's why I'm calling you. What do you think I should do?"

"Bro," I said, "you're not going to like this, but I think you should be obedient. I think you should do what they ask you to do, but don't do it as unto them. Raise your javelin and reflect the Son. Do it as unto God and not as unto men. Because I think God may have an ambush set up for your situation. If He does, you have to be willing to humble yourself so you can see it happen."

My buddy didn't want to hear it. "Man, don't tell me that! I shouldn't have ever picked up this phone."

"I know," I said. "The advice I'm giving you would be hard for me to follow too. Nothing about it is easy. But I dare you to take the risk of faith and not take the bait."

I didn't know what he'd do for sure, but my friend reached out again a month later, and it was like I was talking to a new man.

"JE, I just got a call," he said.

"From who?"

"One of the governing authorities. They've been watching me these past few weeks, and they've realized that they've seen nothing like what was said about me. They're seeing the total opposite of what I was accused of. Because I've done what they've asked and adhered to the plan, they've been able to tell what's really going on, and now they've turned the investigation on my supervisor."

I told him, "That's a signal from God that the ambush is working. You see smoke in the city?" I asked.

"I see smoke in the city, JE!"

We laughed in relief. The smoke was ascending because my buddy was obedient. He'd humbled himself and stepped back.

The next time he met with the leadership, they told him, "We're making *you* the supervisor starting today. As for your old boss, we've investigated him, and he will be working for you from here on out."

Can God ambush your circumstances suddenly? Instantly? You know He can!

Raise your javelin in obedience, and then you wait and see. God will send a signal to let you know He is working for you, securing the win.

Oh, and don't forget: Joshua didn't put down his javelin "until he had utterly destroyed all the inhabitants of Ai" (verse 26). I'm certain that on that day, he was remembering his mentor, Moses, who had held up the staff through the entire battle against Amalek.

Don't lower that thing until the battle is over and the war is won. Raise your javelin until it's finished.

Finish it.

Finish it.

Finish it.

Amen.

CHAPTER 12

FROM TEST TO TESTIMONY

My mom was alive and well for the forty-second anniversary of our church, Oak Cliff Bible Fellowship, back in 2018. My dad let me preach on that milestone day, and I couldn't help but think about the legacy of both my parents, as well as the original members.

I started by giving honor to my mother, because while everybody has seen the height at which my father flies, he was able to do that only because he wasn't carrying the load by himself. Lois Evans was handling the details at home with all the kids (I have five now, so I know what that is), and also serving as an enduring support in the foundation God was establishing. This included thirty years as the executive director for the Urban Alternative's national and international ministry. She was and still is one of the main reasons there have been no cracks in my dad's ministry.

And of course I paid tribute to my dad, who is not just my pastor but one of my best friends in the whole world. To have an incredible father who is also a great man, a faithful husband, an amazing preacher of the Word—to know that what he is saying is what he is living—has been a testimony for my siblings and me as well as our spouses and kids.

I gave honor to another group of people that day as well: those who had helped and supported my parents along the way. "The only reason we can eat fruit this week," I said, "is because they did the toil of planting the seeds." Standing on that stage, I was standing on their shoulders.

Every God-fearing, Bible-believing church has a testimony, but guess what? Every saint within that church has a testimony too. Whether you've celebrated forty-two years with the Lord or four months, you have a testimony. You have some hindsight on what God has done in your life. Some clarity that lets you look back and testify of His provision. Some story to tell of the sovereignty, providence, and grace that has brought you to where you are today.

As we conclude our *Fighting Your Battles* journey together, let me share one verse that really captures what I'm talking about. This statement, spoken by Joseph near the end of his life, is what I call "a testimony for the ages." It speaks to one of the most critical ways that God empowers His warriors to win: through perseverance. It spells out how God works in the lives of those who trust Him for the long haul, wherever He takes them. You probably know the verse, even if you don't recognize the reference, Genesis 50:20:

> As for you, you meant evil against me, but God meant it for good in order to bring about this present result, to preserve many people alive (NASB 1995).

When Joseph summed up his testimony this way, he was about a hundred years old, and he and his brothers had just buried their father. (Joseph himself died ten years later.) Losing a parent you've loved so much makes you reflect hard on your own life. Looking back on his earthly journey, Joseph was recounting to his brothers that *something bad happened*, but God had turned it around and made it good. God had done this to bring him to the place where he was standing, Pharaoh's palace in Egypt. He'd been placed there in order to preserve a multitude of lives.

God's goal is always to preserve lives. And He uses the chapters of our testimony to do it.

Joseph's words offer 20/20 perspective on what God does in the life of a Christian who stays steadfast. As we're about to see, we may be in the pit part of our story, the dark part, the empty part—but that's no time to quit. Somebody in your future will be counting on your testimony. They will need your experiences with the Lord to make it out of their pit and on toward their placement.

Starting in the Red

Your story is one of God's tangible investments in your life. Most people meet God and want the ledger to start in the black. Most of the time, though, the ledger starts in the red and gradually moves its way to the black. So the fact that somebody you know may be in the red right now doesn't mean God isn't invested in them. By the same principle, when you see someone who has arrived at the palace, who seems like they have made it to their purpose with a great home and a great family and a great career or ministry, don't assume that you know their story. You don't know what God took them through to get them to today. Whatever He has done, I can promise you, they didn't start at the top.

God's plan is to take each of us and our churches and our ministries somewhere purposeful. There are things you have gone through, things you are going through—things you must go through—to move you from the pit to the place of purpose where God wants you. The story of that journey is a testimony, and it will probably sound something like Joseph's: Somebody meant evil against you, but God meant it for good in order to bring about the present result.

From 37 to 50

His brothers knew what he was talking about, and so do we. Going back to Genesis 37, Joseph was one of twelve sons, and yet he had special favor from his father, Jacob, as "the son of his old age" (verse 3). Jacob signified this by giving Joseph a multicolored tunic, or as we were told in Sunday school, "a coat of many colors." That robe represented dominion and authority and communicated that Joseph had been handed rights—firstborn rights—even though he wasn't Jacob's firstborn. Joseph was the firstborn of his *mother*, Rachel, who had only two children: him and his brother Benjamin. But they were the youngest of all of Jacob's sons.

Joseph had two things at age seventeen, which is where Genesis 37 picks up: He had external evidence of his father's favor (the robe) and he had a dream. As a visionary, he dreamed of how high he would go. And as one of the babies of the family, he dreamed of his older brothers bowing down to him one day. The problem was, nobody gave his brothers the memo that favor ain't fair. Nobody informed them that things don't always get portioned out equally when it comes to family. So when they saw that tunic and they heard Joseph's dream, they were jealous to the point of outrage. What did they do to try to even the score? Verses 23-24 say that his brothers stripped Joseph of his robe and threw him in a pit.

In one day, Joseph went from being wrapped in his father's favor to being stripped of the evidence of it. He went from walking about freely to being held prisoner.

Recounting the events of Genesis 37, his life as a young man, while he's standing at Genesis 50 as an old man, he admits, "This thing started bad." The people he thought he could tell his dream to were jealous of the very dream that he had. The people he thought would propel him toward his dream were the ones who wanted to deprive him of his dream. That's starting in the red, friends.

Why did his brothers strip Joseph of the robe from their father? Because they couldn't reach into his brain and rip out his dream. That's what they really wanted to do. As a next resort, they tore off the symbol of favor and put him in a pit, hoping his dream would never see the light of day.

This is a tactic of Satan's: Our enemy comes "to steal and kill and destroy" (John 10:10). He'll target your testimony just as quickly as he'll target you. He tries to take your testimony by stripping you of the Father's obvious favor in your life. If he can make you think you've lost favor, then maybe you'll *speak* as if you've lost it. Before you know it, you're *living* like it's gone too.

The external stripping often gets an internal result like that. "My life is worthless. God isn't doing anything with my story." If Satan can get your heart and mind stuck in the pit, that's where you'll stay. That's what your identity will be. He is all about robbing you of your Genesis 50 experience.

This was Satan's goal with Job. Satan took Job's house. He took his family. He afflicted him with boils on his skin. He used all these external methods, applied all these external pressures, with the intent of an internal result: that Job would denounce God. (If you want another example of biblical perseverance, check out his story in the book of Job.) The enemy did it with Adam and Eve. "You see this fruit? You see that tree?" He got them thinking about the external, but the purpose was internal: so that they would sin, denying God.

Satan tried it with Jesus too, although unsuccessfully (see Matthew 4). He showed Jesus some rocks—"Go ahead and turn them into bread." He took Him to the top of the temple in Jerusalem—"Throw Yourself down; the angels will catch You." He showed Him the kingdoms of this earth—"I'll give them to You, but You'll have to bow down and worship me." He is always trying to do something in our external world to deprive us of what God is doing inside us.

This also happened to Oak Cliff Bible Fellowship. Most people don't know that there was a time when we had nowhere to go. We were meeting at Adell Turner Elementary School, and the school had decided they couldn't host us anymore. This put my parents and the elders and deacons between a rock and a hard place. They'd believed we had the Father's favor. They'd seen the Father clearly working, only to watch the enemy strip them of the evidence.

However, the enemy's stripping doesn't mean God no longer has us. Losing the evidence of favor doesn't mean you've lost the providence of God.

Joseph's testimony gives us the perspective we need. The enemy would love to ruin your Genesis 50 testimony...

I'm never going to make it out of here!
I'm not so sure God has my back after all.
Does God even care? Maybe He's forgotten me.

Whatever is going on with you, though, whatever pit you may be in, God is up to something. God is up to something! Don't give up!

The Lord gives every believer a testimony and a purpose. There's nothing random or pointless about the things you go through or the challenges you face. You are not on this planet, or in any pit, just to sit, sulk, and sour.

My mom sure had some stories to tell. She worked in the family sweat factory, our garage, for years. We called it that because there was no air conditioner in there—it was Texas hot in the summers. But she was trying to help my dad get where God was taking the ministry, and so she would call my sisters into the sweat factory to help her put sermon tapes (cassette tapes, y'all!) in envelopes to mail all over the world. So don't think that my parents didn't start with some pit experiences. The "palace" that the ministry is in now, by comparison, is the result of a long journey with God from Genesis 37 to Genesis 50.

God Is Good

Rather than lingering on the rough times, repeating all the difficult details, Joseph moves his testimony along, emphasizing the ending: "You meant evil against me, but God meant it for good in order to bring about this present result, to preserve many people alive" (50:20 NASB 1995).

Did you notice that when God shows up, there is usually a contrasting conjunction? "It was bad, *but God...*" Things change upon His arrival. You get to experience His nature. Mark 10:18 says, "No one is good but God alone" (NRSV).

At the mention of His goodness, people often ask, "But if God is so good, then why do I experience this much bad?" Well, because experiencing the bad is what illuminates that He is good.

Have you ever seen a superhero movie without a villain or any problems? I hope not, because that's dumb—nobody wants a superhero movie where the dude is just flying around, flexing his power. He needs to be able to fix something, make it better. We know we serve a real-life Superhero because we've seen Him in action. We've seen Him redirect evil intent and foil our enemy's plans, turning bad into blessing.

He is a meaning changer. A true transformer. Both phrases in Genesis 50, "meant evil" and "meant...good," speak of the same Genesis 37 experience. But God completely altered what that experience meant. He enters in and transforms our problems to praise. He also positions us for purpose. Let me show you how He did that with Joseph.

Joseph was stripped in Genesis 37, but by chapter 41—starting at verse 42—we see Pharaoh setting him back up with deluxe treatment:

- He took off his signet ring and gave it to Joseph.
- He clothed Joseph with a royal robe.
- He put a fancy necklace, probably weighed down with gold and jewels, around Joseph's neck.
- He had Joseph ride in his second chariot, with messengers announcing his arrival.

These gestures symbolized that Joseph shared the authority of Pharaoh. When Joseph walked into a room or rode down the street, people bowed their knee.

Other people probably looked at him and saw a lucky guy being put in a palace. But what they saw as lucky, Joseph recognized as a loving God positioning him to carry out a very intentional purpose.

Do you see what happened? Joseph had dreams that got him stripped. But with God, that same dream got him equipped.

You realize, don't you, that nobody can really strip you of what God has for you? But God may allow you to be stripped so He can have *you* before He gives you what He has. If He lets you endure a stripping, He's trying to position you for a future equipping.

When you're down to nothing, it's only because God is up to something. As you persevere with Him, God will allow your tests to bring you to your testimony. So don't let the strip make you quit! If my parents had given up because Adell Turner was taken from them, Oak Cliff wouldn't be in the building it is right now, preserving people's lives.

After forty-five years of OCBF going strong, we've learned that the enemy's attempt to strip doesn't mean the Lord's favor is lost. It just means your favor got the enemy's attention. And if you think about it, there's really no better time for God to work some wonders than when He has people's attention.

Turned for Good

It's so important to understand that losing the physical evidence of favor doesn't mean you've lost the spiritual providence of God. I remember my dad telling me that when the school was no longer available as a place for the church to meet, he went to talk to former Cowboy linebacker Bob Breunig at his office. They were great friends, and I can imagine Dad explaining to Bob what had happened: "We no longer have a place to meet; the church is homeless."

While the two of them were talking, some guy walked past the open door—and then he backed up and stood in the doorway. My dad kept looking over his shoulder like, *Who is this guy being nosy?* You know that feeling. When somebody is in your stuff, you want to say, "What are you doing? Keep moving, buddy!" But the dude in the doorway didn't stop at standing there. He got comfortable, crossing one leg over the other, still listening.

Pretty soon, Mr. Nosy comes and sits down beside my dad. At this point, smoke starts coming out of Dad's ears because he's trying to explain to Bob what's going on with the church, and this stranger is butting in. Not only that, the guy starts asking questions. So my dad is giving him short answers: "Yes...no...We're considering that"—all the time wondering, *Why are you here?* The dude is probing him for information, and finally Dad tells him, "There is this little chapel right down the street...We've been talking to the owners about it, but we just don't have the money, so we're trying to figure out what to do."

That's when the stranger asks, "How much does it cost?"

"Two hundred thousand."

Right then and there, that man pulls out his checkbook and

opens it up, and instantly my father's countenance changes. All of a sudden he's answering any and all questions and popping his suit, trying to tell this stranger the whole story. "You know, my bigger vision is to have all the land…" Then Tony Evans starts doing his sermon kicks—he gets up and is stepping around as he talks. And that stranger, he wrote a check on the spot for two hundred thousand dollars and handed it to my father. Then the guy who used to be a nuisance got up out of his seat and walked off into the hallway, his business finished.

Our church has a testimony. So does yours, I'm sure. And so does your life and mine. God will allow you to be stripped, but it's so that He can show up and do some equipping. Some positioning. Some purposing. It's so that you can talk about the goodness of God and how He relocated you from the pit to the palace. You sure didn't get here on your own two feet! Don't forget that. You got here because of God's mercy and grace. You got here because He brought you here.

Sure enough, when my dad cashed that check, it went through. Because when God comes through, His blessings don't bounce. So I want to use our church's testimony, and Joseph's testimony, to encourage you in your testimony. You can't quit in the pit. You can't give up. You've got to know and believe and trust that this good God of ours wants to use that bad scenario of yours to bring you to the pinnacle that He has been preparing you for.

A whole lot of things happen prior to our promotion because God is serious about preparation. You'll be promoted in the challenges you face as you're being promoted in the calling to the race.

Many Christians are trying to press the EASY button, hoping to avoid challenges. While you're trying to have an easy climb, God wants you winning in the hardest places.

Look at it this way. In every sport, the higher you climb toward that championship, the harder it is to win the next game. In football, the NFC or AFC Championship game is tougher and more competitive than all the other games that preceded it. The challenge is greater because the promotion is greater. This is also God's way of delivering greater hope. A championship can be won only if bigger challenges are conquered.

Being really ready for the success God has for you, for the calling and destiny that He has prepared for you, has everything to do with you winning your time in the pit. Persevering with God when things are tough deepens your level of trust in Him.

Open to the Evidence

You've got the stripping/equipping part of Joseph's story down. Good. Now I want to show you another way that God took Joseph's problem and turned it for good. Genesis 37:24 says, "The pit was empty, without any water in it."

That detail made me think. *Now why in the world would the biblical writer go to so much trouble to tell us the nature of the pit?* Normally it would be enough to know that Joseph was in there and how he got there. So why are we being told that it was empty and had no water?

I prayed about that question for three days. (Sometimes we have to read the Bible and then step back and think on it a little bit.) What was the correlation between not just the stripping, and not just the pit, but a pit like this? Why did it have to be empty? Why couldn't it contain any water?

If truth be told, some of you have this question too, only it's personal. You're feeling like *you're* not getting the simplest provision either, and it doesn't make sense. It's insult and injury combined. God seems cruel to put you through such scarcity. But let me pass along to you the insight that I believe the Holy Spirit gave me: *God prepares you for how He is about to use you.*

Let me explain.

In Genesis 41, Joseph translated Pharaoh's dreams that a famine was coming. Pharaoh, seeing that there wasn't another man in the land who had the Spirit of God in him like Joseph did (verse 38), put him in charge of famine preparedness for the entire nation. A famine means people are experiencing emptiness—no food and no water. God didn't want Joseph just having the information: *Oh, there will be no food or water.* He let Joseph experience what that feels like to prepare him for his future purpose in the palace. You see, when you preserve somebody's life, you need to be able to sympathize with their weaknesses. So God had Joseph in a waterless, empty pit, positioning him to compassionately lead a people who would one day be desperately hungry and thirsty.

If someone you know is struggling with addiction, it's nice that you can talk to them from a book, but it's even better if you've been freed of addiction yourself. People want to know that you feel their pain. If somebody has a falling out in their family, your school degree in family therapy can come in handy, but it's even better if your own family has been put back together by God's power. Knowledge is one thing. Life experience takes your ministry to a whole new level of impact. Joseph was using all the things he learned in his past for the future. He went from test to testimony, and so can you.

God intends to use you in specific ways, and you can get a hint of how He will do that by keeping your eyes open in the pit. He will always give you evidence in your struggle. Most people get so focused on the pit itself that they aren't seeing the path to the future. Yet have you ever noticed that your passion to help somebody comes from the very thing that you've struggled with? Look at your life. Hasn't your greatest ministry come from your greatest misery? That's God's thing. It's His trademark. You can always know that God is going to use what you're going through to preserve others' lives.

He isn't just serious about preparation. He's serious about

redemption, wanting no experience to slip through our hands. If we'll let Him work His wonders, God even continues to redeem our past after we've been promoted.

What will stop you is if you decide to sit in the pit, waiting for the Lord to change things for your own purpose. For your throne. Your acclaim. If that's you, I have four words for you: *You ain't the King!* This is for God and His glory. Those of us who have a testimony today can testify, not because we haven't been stripped, but because we kept going and let God equip. He put us in this place, purposed us for it, empowered us to persevere, and now it's time to tell what He has done.

God Is That Good

One of the ways Joseph testified was in the naming of his son. In Genesis 41:51, we read that the boy was named Manasseh, which means "God has made me forget all my trouble and all of my father's household." Hold on. You forgot, Joseph? You don't remember what you went through?

He did remember, based on his statement to his brothers in Genesis 50: "You meant evil against me." So Joseph didn't exactly *forget* as we think of that word—it's not that his cognitive capacity failed; it's just that where he was, it was so plush. God had brought him to a place that was so good, nothing about Joseph's previous placement could taint his current position. Naming his child according to the turn of his testimony was just another way to say so. He didn't name the boy Pain or Pit. Joseph named him I Don't Remember the Bad Stuff.

I once asked my mom about those sweat-factory days, and I commented on how I got the best position in the house: baby of the family. The hardest parts of building a ministry were over by the time I came along.

Mom admitted, "Yeah, those days were tough, but now we have a ministry that pumps out resources so much faster than we ever could back then. Now we're on a thousand stations in over a hundred countries. Now I'm in this air-conditioned building that we own, and I've been able to help lead an international ministry for thirty years."

She wasn't bragging. That was gratitude coming through. That was testimony. My mom was putting God's goodness into words.

When God shows up and takes you out of the pit, He helps you forget some of the pain. You get a little amnesia. Not because you can't recall what happened, but because He's just that good.

I witnessed this with my wife as well.

Having our first child was something. *Ah, sweet Kelsey.* Now I know why my dad used me in illustrations all the time—easy pickings! Anyway, we induced with Kelsey about a week before her due date because the doctor said she was going to be a big baby. And sure enough, she came out at 8 pounds, 8 ounces. If we had waited a week, she would've been 9 pounds. (Our two sons were 9.5 and 9.1.) So, we don't play any games in our household when it comes to delivering babies!

With Kelsey, once my wife and I signed in at the hospital on induction day, we were brought to the delivery room, where Kanika was given her medication. We know now, Kanika doesn't need any medicine because her labors are quick. Our fourth child, Kylar, from the start of labor to the delivery, was ninety minutes! I mean, she was *like a bullet*! But with the first one, we didn't know.

The medication they gave my wife to induce her had a negative effect: Kanika started having contractions with no breaks. *Mmm hmm! I can hear all you ladies who have had babies talking at the pages of this book, sympathizing with my wife.* Kanika's contractions would get worse, and then back off just a little, and then start up again almost immediately. She went through this for a few hours, with very little chance to catch her breath until the doctors were able to figure out a solution to slow down the contractions.

Finally, after sixteen hours, the baby came, and my wife and I were really happy but utterly exhausted, you know? It was such an ordeal that I had already shut down any thoughts of another kid. I was sure that, because of the experience we'd just had, we were done. No way my wife was going to want to do that again. But about ten months later, Kanika came to me and said, "I'm ready for number two."

"Huh?" I was shocked and wasn't sure I heard her right. "But don't you remember what happened with the first one?"

"I remember," she said, "but look at our baby, our sweet Kelsey!"

What she was looking at overruled what she remembered about the pain of childbirth. So I asked, "Are you sure you want to do this?"

"I'm sure."

Now I started getting excited, because while she was telling me she wanted another child, I knew what that meant for me. So I was like—*Hey, I'm ready whenever you're ready, babe! Just give me the word!*

When God delivers what He's going to deliver in your life, you look at that baby and your testimony changes. Joseph said, "It turned out so good that I can't even remember the troubles I had in my father's household."

God is doing something in your life, my brother. He is birthing something in you, my sister. Don't you quit! Don't you wave the white flag in the middle of your pit! You may have lost some of the physical evidence of the Father's favor, but *physical evidence never overrides God's providence*. So don't stay down, thinking you're where you belong. You've got to keep trusting the Lord and persevering in faith with your eyes wide open. Because somebody's life is going to be saved by your testimony.

Let me tell you a little more about my testimony. I played football at Duncanville High, won the state championship, went to Baylor on a full ride, got educated. And all that time, I had a dream to play in the NFL.

On draft day, I was picked up by the Dallas Cowboys. That was a big day for me! But three weeks in, I was stripped. The assistant coach who always delivered the bad news didn't say a word to me. He just pulled the playbook from my hands and pointed to the exit. I knew exactly what that meant: I was going back where I came from.

While being drafted by Dallas had been a dream come true, it's not like I had a few hours on a plane to mope about being cut and collect my thoughts. No, I only had twenty minutes because that's how soon I'd be home.

Not long after, I got a call from the San Diego Chargers. They wanted me playing in NFL Europe in the spring before joining them in the fall for the NFL season back in the US. I felt a new sense of hope. *Okay, God, let's make this thing happen! Let's see this dream come to life!*

At NFL Europe training camp (held in Tampa, of all places), things went downhill—and then they just kept going that way. You practice for two hours in the extreme heat, and they let you take off your helmet long enough to eat a banana and an apple and get some water, and then you put in another two-hour practice. I was already feeling like it wasn't for me, that I couldn't handle all this stripping.

One day, I'd had enough. It seemed like every ounce of favor was gone. So I called my dad and told him, "I'm out. I'm quitting football and coming home."

"Are you sure, son?"

"I'm really sure."

While my dad was booking the ticket, I went to the coach's office. "I'm going home," I told him.

"We don't want you going home, JE. You're a good player."

My literal words were, "I don't care what you want. I'm going home right now." That was frustrated, twenty-two-year-old Jonathan Evans talking.

Coach kept his cool. "You can't leave right now; you need your exit physical first. That's a liability for us otherwise. We let a player go home before that, and he can come back and say 'I was hurt on the job,' and try to get paid that way. You can do your physical tomorrow and leave tomorrow night."

So I called my dad back. "I can't come home till tomorrow night."

"Don't you think it's interesting—"

I cut him off. "Oh, Lord, here goes the philosopher!"

But he kept right on going, "...that you couldn't leave when you wanted to leave?" Then he flipped into negotiator mode, "So I want you to do something for me. I want you to go to one more practice and I want you to ask God if He wants you there in spite of whether you think you want to be there."

I did what my dad said, though I kid you not, I cried during that practice. You know how you can't control your neck because you're crying so hard? My neck was cocking back, and I couldn't do anything about it. Because I didn't want to be there. It was a pit for me. An absolute pit experience. Still, I said to God, "If You want me here, then You'll have to give me a peace that surpasses all understanding." And, this is no exaggeration, the next time I put my hand in the dirt for the next snap—I felt completely different! As soon as I made the play, I turned to my coach and said, "I'm staying."

He said, "Okay, great!"

A couple of weeks later, after the training camp in Tampa was over, our team flew to Germany to start the NFL Europe season. That place was white walls, white sheets, and no English-speaking TV channels. For months! But by the end of the season, my teammates had given me a new nickname. They called me "Rev," short for Reverend. Seven players accepted Jesus as Savior.

Now I felt like I knew the exchange God was requiring. If I prayed with guys and led them to the Lord, He was going to let me run out of an NFL tunnel and live the game day dream. I was young, trying to manipulate God to put me at the pinnacle where I saw myself. *Great doing business with You, God.*

But no. I go to the Tennessee Titans. I get cut. I go to the Washington Redskins. I get cut. This was all between 2005, when I was drafted, and 2009. Finally, in 2011, I was standing in the tunnel with the Dallas Cowboys, waiting for my first regular-season game. Not as a player but as the team's chaplain. God turned my misery within the game of football into my ministry within the game of football.

The Turnaround

God has a plan and a place for your testimony. It may not be your plan or your definition of a palace, but it's a good plan and a good place. And it will be revealed from the trials and tests, the battles and bruises, the pits and perils that you go through in this life. He's provided you with your entire story to give you a future and a hope—and someone else as well. You've been positioned and purposed to preserve somebody's life by the blood of the Lamb and the word of your testimony.

We have a testimony because Jesus had a testimony. In the plan of the Father and the resurrecting power of the Holy Spirit, Jesus defeated the evil that Satan meant against all of us, and Jesus now sits enthroned as King of kings and Lord of lords in the palace of heaven. Now that's a turnaround!

Jesus made our triumph happen—He saved us through His testimony.

You may be feeling like you're in a pit so deep, you'll never get out. You may be feeling like the favor of God is so long gone, you'll never have it back. But look for the evidence. Trust what He is doing. And persevere in faith. As you live your story, you'll be able to tell your story. And lives will be saved because of it. Others will someday praise Him because you testified. They will come to know Him because they heard of His goodness through you. They will trust Him to the end because you trusted Him first.

The pit is just the beginning of your story. Be steadfast, will you? The testimony from your test is coming. Persevere, for your victory is near.

Scan the QR code or visit
https://jonathanblakeevans.com/fyb-film-4/
to download your "Fighting Your Battles" soundtrack now!
(chapters 10–12)

SCRIPTURE VERSIONS USED IN THIS BOOK

To learn more about Harvest House books and
to read sample chapters, visit our website:

www.HarvestHousePublishers.com

HARVEST HOUSE PUBLISHERS
EUGENE, OREGON